Eggs

Eggs

Nourishing recipes
for health and wellness

This edition published by Parragon Books Ltd in 2016 and distributed by

Parragon Inc.
440 Park Avenue South, 13th Floor
New York, NY 10016
www.parragon.com/lovefood

LOVE FOOD is an imprint of Parragon Books Ltd

ISBN: 978-1-4748-1771-4

Printed in China

Cover photography by Tony Briscoe
New recipes by Teresa Goldfinch
New recipe photography by Kris Kirkham
New home economy by Lucy-Ruth Hathaway

Notes for the Reader
This book uses standard kitchen measuring spoons and cups. All spoon and cup measurements are level unless otherwise indicated. Unless otherwise stated, milk is assumed to be whole, eggs are large, individual vegetables and fruits are medium, and pepper is freshly ground black pepper. A pinch of salt is calculated as $\frac{1}{16}$ of a teaspoon. Unless otherwise stated, all root vegetables should be peeled prior to using.

Garnishes, decorations, and serving suggestions are all optional and not necessarily included in the recipe ingredients or method. Any optional ingredients and seasoning to taste are not included in the nutritional analysis.

The times given are only an approximate guide. Preparation times differ according to the techniques used by different people and the cooking times may also vary from those given. Optional ingredients, variations, or serving suggestions have not been included in the time calculations.

While the publisher of the book and the original author(s) of the recipes and other text have made all reasonable efforts to ensure that the information contained in this book is accurate and up to date at the time of publication, anyone reading this book should note the following important points:

Medical and pharmaceutical knowledge is constantly changing and the author(s) and the publisher cannot and do not guarantee the accuracy or appropriateness of the contents of this book;

In any event, this book is not intended to be, and should not be relied upon, as a substitute for appropriate, tailored professional advice. Both the author(s) and the publisher strongly recommend that a physician or other healthcare professional is consulted before embarking on major dietary changes;

For the reasons set out above, and to the fullest extent permitted by law, the author(s) and publisher: (i) cannot and do not accept any legal duty of care or responsibility in relation to the accuracy or appropriateness of the contents of this book, even where expressed as "advice" or using other words to this effect; and (ii) disclaim any liability, loss, damage, or risk that may be claimed or incurred as a consequence—directly or indirectly—of the use and/or application of any of the contents of this book.

For best results, use a food thermometer when cooking meat. Check the latest government guidelines for current advice.

Contents

Introduction

Eggs have been an important part of our diet since prehistory. Wild fowl have been domesticated in India as early as 3200 BC, although domesticated chickens have been in Europe since only 600 BC, when jungle fowl native to tropical and subtropical Southeast Asia and India were brought there. Originally quail and ostrich were the main source of eggs. In ancient Rome, eggs were often preserved and then served as a course in their own right. It's believed that the first chickens were taken to the Americas by Columbus on his second voyage there in 1493.

Of course, we now eat more chicken eggs than any other eggs, but it is possible to buy eggs from other species of bird, such as ducks, geese, and quails. Chicken eggs are available year round (thanks to the use of artificial light), but birds normally lay eggs in spring—so this is the season when other eggs are more readily available in the stores.

Common Varieties & Breeds

CHICKEN

There are many breeds of chicken. Not only are they raised intensively by the poultry industry, but these birds are popular among backyard chicken enthusiasts. Breeds may be chosen for the eggs they lay. A heavy breed (such as Rhode Island Red) produces darker brown eggs, while a light breed (such as the White Leghorn) lay white or light-colored eggs. Some breeds are selected for their large eggs; others, for a greater number of smaller eggs. Breeds may also be chosen because they are hardy—they can thrive in cold weather. Standard chicken egg sizes vary from small to jumbo (1½–2½ ounces), with a large egg (2 ounces) being the standard egg size used in recipes. Bantams, a small chicken breed, lay eggs at only 1–1½ ounces. These have a dark yolk and a 50:50 ratio of yolk to white, which is much higher than that of a standard chicken egg.

DUCK

The larger, duck eggs tend to weigh 3–3¼ ounces. Their higher fat content and light, creamy yolks make them richer than chicken eggs.

GOOSE

The translucent ivory shell of these eggs is unique, as is their size. They weigh in at 6¼–7 ounces each, making them really substantial. One goose egg is the equivalent of 2½ large chicken eggs. The flavor is rich and creamy.

QUAIL

These tiny eggs are one-quarter of the size of chicken eggs and are cute. Their small speckled shells contain delicate eggs with pale yolks. It takes just 30 seconds to soft boil them and they're perfect for canapés.

THE LESS WELL-KNOWN

There are also some less well-known eggs that, if you can find them, will add a little wow factor to any dinner party.

Unlike chicken eggs, these may not be available year round, and you may have to search for them in gourmet food stores or online.

Why not seek out rhea eggs? The rhea is a bird that closely resembles an ostrich and provides large eggs that are light and fluffy and highly versatile. You could try an actual ostrich egg, but be sure you allow enough time to cook them, because they can take 50 minutes simply to soft boil and a somewhat lengthy 2 hours to hard boil.

Another overlooked egg type is that from the guinea fowl, which is small and delicate. You can also try pheasant eggs, which have beautiful olive-green and brown shells and a rich flavor.

Perfect Eggs

The benefits of eating eggs cannot be overestimated. A large chicken egg contains around 70 calories and is a good source of all the essential nutrients. Eggs contain high-quality protein, the macronutrient that best satisfies hunger. They also contain essential vitamins, including vitamin A, needed for healthy skin and good vision; vitamin D, which is deficient in many people's diets; vitamin E, which may help reduce the incidence of heart disease, certain cancers, and strokes; and the B vitamins. Vitamin B2 is needed for metabolizing food and vitamin B12 helps brain function and provides energy. B12 is often lacking in the diet of vegetarians and older people.

Eggs also contain essential minerals, such as phosphorous, which is essential for strong bones and teeth; iodine, which is important for thyroid function; and selenium, which is thought to protect against certain cancers. They also contain trace elements, including iron, which helps with red blood cell formation, and zinc, which supports the immune system.

The protein in eggs is extremely high quality and is a "complete" protein. This means that it contains all eight of the essential amino acids. Its quality is comparable to that of beef or milk and is easily digestible. Some eggs now contain omega-3 fatty acids, depending on what the chickens have been fed—always check the packaging to be sure.

Eggs were once criticized for their high cholesterol content but this has reduced in recent times with improvements in chicken feed. It's now been shown that saturated fat in the diet has the greatest impact on blood cholesterol levels.

EGG SAFETY

Eating raw eggs or eggs with runny yolks, or any food containing uncooked, lightly cooked, or raw eggs can cause food poisoning. This is especially important for anyone in an "at risk" group, such as:

• Babies and toddlers
• The elderly
• Pregnant women
• People with a weak immune system.

This is because eggs may contain salmonella bacteria, which can cause serious illness.

People who do not belong to one of the at risk categories and eat foods containing lightly cooked eggs should not experience any health problems, but cooking eggs thoroughly is always the safest option if you are concerned about food poisoning.

Breakfast & Snacks

HEALTHY BREAKFAST FRITTATA 13

EGG WHITE OMELET 14

ASPARAGUS, SALMON & POACHED EGG 17

HAM & EGG CUPS 19

POACHED EGGS & KALE WITH SOURDOUGH 20

KNOW YOUR EGGS 22

DUCK EGGS BENEDICT 25

CHIVE SCRAMBLED EGGS WITH BRIOCHE 26

POLENTA CAKES WITH POACHED EGGS 29

MUSHROOM & EGG CUPS 30

TEA-SOAKED EGGS 33

CHORIZO & QUAIL EGG TOASTS 34

DEVILED EGGS 37

SPICY OVEN-BAKED SAUSAGE-COATED EGGS 39

PERFECT PICKLED EGGS 40

Healthy Breakfast Frittata

Serve this frittata straight from the pan with homemade whole wheat bread, or wrap it in wax paper and aluminum foil and enjoy it cold at work.

SERVES:	PREP: *15 mins*	PER SERVING: *241 cals* | *15.1g fat* | *3.5g sat fat* | *13.7g carbs* | *2.6g sugar*
4	COOK: *20 mins*	*2.9g fiber* | *13.2g protein* | *440mg sodium*

INGREDIENTS

8 ounces small new potatoes, unpeeled and
sliced
2 tablespoons virgin olive oil
4 scallions, thinly sliced
1 zucchini, thinly sliced
4 cups baby spinach, trimmed
large pinch of smoked hot paprika
6 eggs
sea salt and pepper (optional)

1. Bring a saucepan of water to a boil, add the potatoes, and cook for 5 minutes, or until just tender, then drain well.

2. Meanwhile, heat 1 tablespoon of oil in a large ovenproof skillet over medium heat. Add the scallions, zucchini, and potatoes and sauté, stirring and turning the vegetables, for 5 minutes, or until just beginning to brown.

3. Add the spinach and paprika and cook, stirring, for 1–2 minutes, or until the leaves have just wilted.

4. Preheat the broiler to medium–hot. Crack the eggs into a bowl and season to taste with salt and pepper, if using. Beat lightly with a fork until evenly mixed. Pour a little extra oil into the pan, if needed, then pour in the eggs and cook for 5–6 minutes, or until they are almost set and the underside of the frittata is golden brown.

5. Broil the frittata for 3–4 minutes, or until the top is browned and the eggs are set. Cut into wedges and serve immediately.

WHY NOT TRY

This versatile dish also makes a satisfying lunch or main meal. Serve with a crisp salad or steamed vegetables of your choice.

Egg White Omelet

Separate the whites from the yolks to make this healthy breakfast omelet with bell peppers and goat cheese, perfect by itself or as an accompaniment to a more hearty breakfast.

SERVES: 1	PREP: *20 mins* COOK: *12–14 mins*	PER SERVING: *146 cals* | *9.4g fat* | *6.2g sat fat* | *3.7g carbs* | *1.8g sugar* *1.3g fiber* | *11g protein* | *760mg sodium*

INGREDIENTS

¼ red bell pepper, seeded
2 extra-large egg whites
1 scallion, thinly sliced
pinch of salt
pinch of black pepper
1 spray of vegetable or olive oil spray
1 ounce fresh goat cheese
2 teaspoons chopped fresh basil,
  plus 3 extra sprigs, to garnish
1 tablespoon snipped fresh chives,
  to garnish

1. Preheat the broiler. Put the red bell pepper on a baking pan under the broiler, skin side up, and roast until it begins to blacken. Remove and place in a plastic bag or a bowl covered with plastic wrap and set aside until cool enough to handle. Discard the blackened skin and dice the bell pepper.

2. In a small bowl, mix together the egg whites, scallion, salt, and black pepper, stirring to combine well.

3. Coat a skillet with the vegetable or olive oil spray and heat over medium heat. Add the egg mixture and cook for about 3 minutes or until the egg is set, turning the skillet frequently and running a spatula around the edge to maintain a thin, even layer of egg.

4. Crumble the goat cheese in a strip down the center of the omelet, then top with the diced bell pepper and the basil. Fold the sides over the filling and slide the omelet onto a plate. Serve immediately, garnished with basil and chives.

TRY SOMETHING DIFFERENT
Replace the red bell pepper with sliced chestnut mushrooms.
Cook the mushrooms over a high heat for 5 minutes before
adding to the cooked omelet with the goat cheese.

Asparagus, Salmon & Poached Egg

Perfect your poached egg skills and serve on top of a bed of salmon and asparagus for a light, fresh, and delicious breakfast.

SERVES:	PREP: *20–25 mins, plus chilling*
2	COOK: *26–28 mins*

PER SERVING: *702 cals | 52.4g fat | 19g sat fat | 6.3g carbs | 1.8g sugar 1.8g fiber | 52.6g protein | 1480mg sodium*

INGREDIENTS

4 tablespoons unsalted butter, softened

finely grated zest of ½ unwaxed lemon, plus ½ teaspoon juice

sprig of fresh dill, coarsely chopped

1 pound hot-smoked salmon

10 asparagus spears, woody stems removed

2 extra-large eggs

sea salt and pepper (optional)

1. Preheat the oven to 350°F. Put the butter, lemon zest and juice, and dill into a small bowl, season to taste with salt and pepper, if using, and mix. Pat the butter into a coarse square with the back of a spoon, wrap it in plastic wrap, and chill in the refrigerator while you make the rest of the dish.

2. Wrap the hot-smoked salmon in aluminum foil and bake for 15 minutes. Flake the fish into bite-size pieces and keep warm.

3. Cook the asparagus in a saucepan of lightly salted boiling water for 2 minutes. Drain and put under cold running water briefly to stop the cooking process, then set aside.

4. Heat a wide saucepan of water until it is almost at simmering point. Crack one egg into a cup, then stir the water to make a whirlpool. As the whirlpool slows almost to a stop, gently slip the egg into its center. Cook for 2–3 minutes, then remove with a slotted spoon. Repeat with the second egg.

5. Put five asparagus spears on each of two plates, top with half the flaked salmon, then balance a poached egg on top and finish off with a dab of lemon butter. Serve immediately.

TOP TIP

The remaining heat from the egg should melt the lemon butter into a delicious lemon herb sauce.

Ham & Egg Cups

These baked eggs look sophisticated but take just minutes to prepare, so breakfast can feel like a special meal any day of the week.

SERVES: 4	PREP: *20 mins* COOK: *15–20 mins*	PER SERVING: *160 cals* | *11g fat* | *4.3g sat fat* | *1.7g carbs* | *0.6g sugar* *0.5g fiber* | *13.5g protein* | *280mg sodium*

INGREDIENTS

1 tablespoon olive oil, for oiling
8 slices wafer-thin ham
1 tablespoon butter
4 scallions, thinly sliced
4 extra-large chicken eggs or 4 duck eggs
pepper (optional)
4 slices hot buttered toast, to serve (optional)

1. Preheat the oven to 400°F. Lightly oil four cups in a muffin pan. Line each cup with 2 slices of ham, laying the slices across one another and ruffling them around the sides to make cups. There will be some ham protruding above the top of the pan.

2. Melt the butter in a small skillet. Add the scallions and gently sauté for 2 minutes, until soft. Remove from the heat. Divide two-thirds of the scallions and their buttery juice among the ham cups.

3. Crack the eggs, one at a time, into a small bowl. Slide into the ham cups, being careful not to let the eggs run down the sides. Season to taste with pepper, if using. Spoon the remaining scallions over the eggs and bake in the preheated oven for 12–15 minutes, until the whites of the eggs are just set. Serve immediately with hot buttered toast.

TRY SOMETHING DIFFERENT

Replace the scallions with a few thinly sliced and sautéed mushrooms, or spoon 1 teaspoon of ketchup into the bottom of each ham cup and sprinkle the eggs with grated cheese before baking.

Poached Eggs & Kale with Sourdough

Kale adds valuable nutrients and vivid green color to these protein-packed poached eggs served on sensational sourdough toast.

SERVES:	PREP: *20 mins*
4	COOK: *15–17 mins*

PER SERVING: *324 cals* | *15.1g fat* | *3g sat fat* | *36.3g carbs* | *2.6g sugar* | *4.4g fiber* | *12.6g protein* | *400mg sodium*

INGREDIENTS

4 eggs
3½ oz kale, chopped
4 large slices of whole-wheat sourdough bread
2 garlic cloves, halved
2 tablespoons olive oil
1 teaspoon crushed red pepper flakes
salt and pepper (optional)

1. Begin by poaching the eggs. Bring a shallow saucepan of water to a gentle simmer. Crack an egg into a small bowl, then slide the egg into the water, lowering the bowl as close to the water as possible. Using a large spoon, gently fold any stray strands of white around the yolk. Repeat with the other eggs.

2. Cook for 2–3 minutes, or until set to your preference, then remove with a slotted spoon. Place the eggs in a small bowl of warm water so they can sit until needed.

3. Bring a saucepan of water to a boil and add the kale. Simmer for 3–4 minutes, or until the kale is just cooked but still retains a little crunch. Drain, season with salt and pepper, if using, and set aside.

4. Meanwhile, toast the sourdough bread. Place the toast on four plates, then rub each slice with the raw garlic and drizzle with the olive oil. Top the toast with the blanched kale and a poached egg. Finally, sprinkle with crushed red pepper flakes. Serve immediately.

WHY NOT TRY

If you don't have kale you could always use spinach for this recipe. It would also work well topped with scrambled eggs.

Know Your Eggs

The beauty of eggs is their versatility; however short of time you are, they make a perfect and nutritious meal. Just follow a few simple rules and try to use fresh eggs as much as possible.

MASTERING THE BASICS WITH CHICKEN EGGS

Portion size: 2-3 eggs per person

BOILED EGGS (SOFT AND HARD)
Cook in fast boiling water for 3–4 minutes for soft-boiled eggs. For hard-boiled, cook in fast boiling water for 6–7 minutes, then run under cold water for 1 minute after cooking to prevent a dark ring from forming around the yolk.

POACHED EGGS
3½–4 minutes. Do not add salt to the water. Add a little vinegar to help keep the egg whites together (about 3 tablespoons for each 4 cups of water). Cook the eggs in a sauté pan or skillet with about 3 inches of water. To test if the egg is cooked, lift it out with a slotted spoon and lightly press the egg with your fingertip. The white should be set and the yolks should feel soft. If cooking in advance or for a crowd, keep the poached eggs warm in a bowl of warm water—or cold water if using cold in salads. Drain well on clean paper towels before serving.

OMELET
To make a classic folded omelet, simply whisk together 2–3 eggs with some seasoning until light and frothy. Add a little butter to a hot skillet and when it is just beginning to brown add the eggs and stir briskly with a fork for 8–10 seconds, until it begins to thicken. Using a spatula, move the setting egg at the sides of the pan into the center and continue cooking for an additional 15–30 seconds, or until lightly set. Place the cheese or ham on one half of the omelet and continue cooking until the cheese has melted or the ham has warmed through. Increase the heat slightly and cook for an additional 30 seconds, until the omelet is fully set and browned on the bottom. Fold the omelet in half by folding up the side without the filling, slide onto a warm plate, and serve immediately.

PAN-FRIED EGGS
Heat a nonstick skillet with a little oil. Carefully break the egg into a cup and pour into the pan. This will help it to slide into the pan without breaking the yolk. Cook over medium heat for 3–4 minutes, until the egg white is firm but the yolk is still soft. If you prefer, flip the egg during cooking to cook both sides.

SCRAMBLED EGGS
2 eggs will take 5–8 minutes; season well, whisk for 1 minute, until frothy, before cooking. Don't add salt until you're ready to cook, or the eggs will be rubbery in texture.

COOKING TECHNIQUE	DUCK EGG	GOOSE EGG	QUAIL EGG
PORTION SIZE	1 egg per person	1 egg for 2-3 people	2-3 eggs per person
SOFT BOILED	6-7 minutes	9-11 minutes	30 seconds
HARD BOILED	9 minutes	13 minutes	1 minute
POACHED	3-5 minutes	9-12 minutes	30 seconds
SCRAMBLED	6-9 minutes	12-15 minutes	not recommended

Duck Eggs Benedict

Here is a delicious twist on a favorite breakfast treat, with crispy pancetta and luxurious duck egg hollandaise sauce.

SERVES:	PREP: *20 mins*	PER SERVING: *389 cals*	*28.4g fat*	*12.4g sat fat*	*15.7g carbs*	*3.2g sugar*
4	COOK: *15 mins*		*0.9g fiber*	*17.1g protein*	*680mg sodium*	

INGREDIENTS

1 teaspoon white wine vinegar
4 fresh duck eggs
8 slices pancetta or dry-cure smoked bacon strips
2 English muffins
softened butter, for spreading (optional)
black pepper (optional)
½ tsp snipped fresh chives, to garnish

HOLLANDAISE SAUCE

1 duck egg yolk
2 teaspoons water
1 teaspoon lemon juice
4 tablespoons butter, melted and cooled slightly
salt (optional)
pinch of cayenne pepper

1. To make the hollandaise sauce, put the egg yolk, water, and lemon juice into a heatproof bowl and whisk until pale and foamy. Place the bowl over a saucepan of barely simmering water and continue whisking for 1–2 minutes, until the egg is slightly thickened.

2. Remove the bowl from the pan, then pour in the butter in a thin stream, whisking continuously to make a light smooth sauce—stop pouring before you reach the milk solids in the bottom of the pan. Season to taste with salt, if using, and a pinch of cayenne pepper. Keep warm over the pan of hot water with the heat turned off until ready to serve.

3. Preheat the broiler. Fill a wide saucepan halfway with water, heat until simmering, then add the vinegar. Crack the eggs into a cup, one at a time, and gently slide into the water. Poach for 3 minutes. Remove with a slotted spoon and drain well on paper towels.

4. Meanwhile, broil the pancetta for 1–2 minutes, until crispy, and chop the slices in half. Halve, toast, and butter the muffins, if desired.

5. Place half a muffin on each plate, divide the pancetta among them, and season with black pepper, if using. Top with the eggs, spoon about 2 tablespoons of the hollandaise sauce over each one, and sprinkle with chives to garnish. Serve immediately.

Chive Scrambled Eggs with Brioche

As a slightly decadent twist on the usual scrambled eggs on toast, add chives and serve on brioche slices for an indulgent start to the day.

SERVES:	PREP: *10 mins*
4	COOK: *6–8 mins*

PER SERVING: *269 cals | 17.8g fat | 9.2g sat fat | 17g carbs | 4.2g sugar 0.6g fiber | 9.7g protein | 240mg sodium*

INGREDIENTS

4 eggs
½ cup light cream
2 tablespoons snipped fresh chives
2 tablespoons butter
4 slices brioche loaf, lightly toasted
salt and pepper (optional)
4 whole fresh chives, to garnish

1. Break the eggs into a medium bowl and whisk gently with the cream. Season to taste with salt and pepper, if using, and add the snipped chives.

2. Melt the butter in a sauté pan and pour in the egg mixture. Let set slightly, then move the mixture toward the center of the pan, using a wooden spoon, as the eggs begin to cook. Continue in this way until the eggs are cooked but still creamy.

3. Place the toasted brioche slices on two warm plates and spoon the scrambled eggs over them. Serve immediately, garnished with whole chives.

TRY SOMETHING DIFFERENT

For a healthier version replace the light cream for skim milk and the butter for cooking oil spray.

Polenta Cakes with Poached Eggs

Don't let the polenta scraps go to waste. You can serve them as an unusual side dish by coarsely chopping and putting them into a shallow ovenproof dish, brushing with melted butter, and broiling for 3 minutes.

SERVES:	PREP: *20 mins, plus cooling*
4	COOK: *15–18 mins*

PER SERVING: *429 cals | 23.9g fat | 11g sat fat | 35g carbs | 0.9g sugar 3g fiber | 18.2g protein | 560mg sodium*

INGREDIENTS

1 tablespoons oil, for oiling
2½ cups water
1 cup cornmeal
1 cup freshly grated Parmesan cheese
3 tablespoons butter
½ red chile, seeded and finely chopped
7 cups baby spinach, or a mixture of baby spinach and arugula
2 teaspoons white wine vinegar
4 extra-large eggs
salt and pepper (optional)

1. Lightly oil a 7-inch square cake pan. Bring the water to a boil in a saucepan. Add the cornmeal in a thin stream and cook, stirring, over medium–low heat for 3 minutes, until thick. Stir in ⅔ cup of the cheese, 2 tablespoons of the butter, and the chile.

2. Working quickly, transfer to the prepared pan and level the surface. Set aside for 30 minutes, until cool and firm, then cut out four circles with a 3½-inch cutter and transfer to a baking pan.

3. Wash the spinach and put into a large saucepan with the water clinging to the leaves. Cover and cook for 2–3 minutes, until wilted, then squeeze out the excess water between two plates. Return to the pan.

4. Preheat the broiler to high. Sprinkle the cornmeal circles with the remaining cheese, place under the preheated broiler, and cook for 3 minutes, until brown and bubbling on the top. Keep the polenta cakes warm. Meanwhile, add the remaining butter to the spinach and heat through.

5. Fill a saucepan halfway with water, add the vinegar, and bring to simmering point. Crack the eggs into cups and slide gently into the water. Cook over low heat, without letting the water boil, for 3 minutes, until the whites are firm and the yolk is still soft. Scoop out with a slotted spoon and drain briefly on paper towels.

6. To serve, place the polenta cakes on four warm plates and divide the spinach among them. Top with the eggs and season to taste with salt and pepper, if using. Serve immediately.

Mushroom & Egg Cups

Here the classic flavors of breakfast—egg, bacon, and mushroom—are combined in a more unusual, yet equally delicious, way.

SERVES:	PREP: *25 mins*
6	COOK: *20–25 mins*

PER SERVING: *418 cals | 18.1g fat | 4.8g sat fat | 49.5g carbs | 3.7g sugar 7.4g fiber | 18.8g protein | 760mg sodium*

INGREDIENTS

2 tablespoons virgin olive oil

2 oak-smoked bacon slices, rind removed, diced

2 cups sliced white button mushrooms

3 eggs

½ cup milk

⅓ cup shredded cheddar cheese

1 tablespoon finely snipped fresh chives

12 cherry tomatoes

sea salt and pepper (optional)

6 slices whole wheat bread, to serve

1. Preheat the oven to 375°F. Line the holes of a six-cup muffin pan with parchment paper. Heat 1 tablespoon of oil in a small skillet over medium–high heat. Add the bacon and cook for 2–3 minutes, or until just beginning to turn golden. Add the mushrooms and sauté, stirring, for 2 minutes. Spoon the mixture into the muffin pan cups.

2. Crack the eggs into a bowl, add the milk, cheddar, and chives, and season with salt and pepper, if using. Beat lightly with a fork until evenly mixed, then pour into the cups of the muffin pan. Stir so the bacon and mushrooms are not all on the bottom of the pan. Bake in the center of the oven for 15 minutes.

3. Put the tomatoes on a baking sheet, drizzle with the remaining oil, and season to taste with salt and pepper, if using. Add to the oven for the last 10 minutes of cooking time. Lightly toast the bread, then cut each slice in half.

4. Lift out the mushroom and egg cups, arrange on plates with the toast and baked tomatoes, and serve immediately.

HELPFUL HINT

Enjoy these baked eggs straight from the oven with hot whole wheat toast and baked tomatoes, or pack in foil with cherry tomatoes for a breakfast to go.

Tea-soaked Eggs

These marinated eggs are a popular Chinese snack food traditionally served during the New Year celebrations. They make an interesting addition to rice and noodle dishes, salads, picnics, and packed lunches.

MAKES:	PREP: *15 mins, plus standing & chilling*	PER EGG: *74 cals* | *4.7g fat* | *1.6g sat fat* | *0.8g carbs* | *0.5g sugar*
6	COOK: *20 mins*	*trace fiber* | *6.4g protein* | *160mg sodium*

INGREDIENTS

6 eggs
2½ cups water
2 black tea bags
2 tablespoons dark soy sauce
2 teaspoons packed light brown sugar
3 star anise
1 small cinnamon stick
½-inch piece fresh ginger, peeled and coarsely chopped

1. Put the eggs into a saucepan just large enough to hold them in a single layer and cover with cold water. Bring to a boil, then remove from the heat. Cover the pan and let stand for 7 minutes. Remove the eggs with a slotted spoon and cool under running water.

2. Using the back of a teaspoon, gently tap the eggs all over to create small cracks in the shells, being careful not to break the membrane underneath.

3. Pour the measured water into the pan. Add the tea bags, soy sauce, sugar, star anise, cinnamon, and ginger. Stir to dissolve the sugar, then return the eggs to the pan. Gently simmer for 15 minutes.

4. Remove from the heat and let cool, then transfer the eggs in their liquid to a bowl. Cover and refrigerate for at least 8 hours or overnight. Drain the eggs and carefully peel off the shells to reveal the pattern underneath.

TOP TIP
If you prefer a stronger flavour, leave the eggs in the marinade for up to 48 hours.

Chorizo & Quail Egg Toasts

Quail's eggs may be smaller in size, but not in flavour. Pair with slices of chorizo for an interesting and flavorsome breakfast, an inventive variation on traditional eggs and bacon.

MAKES:	PREP: *15–20 mins*	PER EGG TOAST: *103 cals* | *3.8g fat* | *1g sat fat* | *12.5g carbs* | *0.7g sugar*
12	COOK: *10–14 mins*	*0.6g fiber* | *4.6g protein* | *200mg sodium*

INGREDIENTS

12 slices French bread, sliced on the diagonal, about ¼ inch thick
12 thin, ready-to-eat chorizo sausage slices
1 tablespoon olive oil
12 quail eggs
¼ teaspoon mild paprika pepper, for dusting
salt and black pepper (optional)

1. Preheat the broiler to high. Arrange the slices of bread on a baking sheet and broil until golden brown on both sides.

2. Cut or fold the chorizo slices to fit on the toasts and set aside.

3. Heat a thin layer of oil in a large skillet over medium heat until a cube of bread browns in 30 seconds. Break the eggs into the skillet and cook, spooning the oil over the yolks, until the whites are set and the yolks are set to your preference.

4. Remove the fried eggs from the skillet and drain on paper towels. Immediately transfer to the chorizo-topped toasts and dust with a pinch of paprika. Sprinkle with salt and black pepper to taste, if using, and serve immediately.

TOP TIP

Despite their delicate appearance, quail eggs can be difficult to crack because of a relatively thick membrane under the shell. It is useful to have a pair of scissors handy to cut through the membrane as you break the eggs into the skillet.

Deviled Eggs

Ideal as an appetizer at a party or simply as a snack, devilled eggs pack a whole host of delicious flavors into just a few mouthfuls.

MAKES:	PREP: *20–25 mins, plus cooling*	PER DEVILLED EGG: *84 cals* | *6.6g fat* | *1.5g sat fat* | *1.7g carbs* | *0.9g sugar*
16	COOK: *15 mins*	*0.5g fiber* | *4.3g protein* | *80mg sodium*

INGREDIENTS

8 extra-large eggs

2 whole canned or bottled pimientos del piquillo

16 pitted green Spanish olives

⅓ cup mayonnaise

8 drops of hot pepper sauce

large pinch of cayenne pepper, plus 1 tsp extra, to garnish

salt and pepper (optional)

16 butterhead lettuce leaves, to serve

1. Put the eggs into a saucepan, cover with cold water, and slowly bring to a boil. Reduce the heat to low, cover, and simmer gently for 10 minutes. Drain the eggs and place under cold running water until they are cold.

2. Crack the eggshells and remove. Halve the eggs lengthwise. Carefully remove the yolks and place them in a strainer set over a bowl and rub through, then mash with a fork.

3. Place the pimientos on paper towels to dry well, then finely chop, reserving 16 small strips.

4. Finely chop half the olives, then halve the remaining olives.

5. Add the chopped pimientos and chopped olives to the mashed egg yolks. Add the mayonnaise, mix together well, then add the hot pepper sauce, cayenne pepper, and season to taste with salt and black pepper, if using.

6. Use a teaspoon to spoon a little of the egg yolk mixture into the hollow in each egg white half.

7. Add a small strip of the reserved pimientos and an olive half to the top of each stuffed egg.

8. Line a plate with lettuce leaves and arrange the eggs on top. Dust with a little paprika and serve.

Spicy Oven-baked Sausage-coated Eggs

These sausage-coated eggs are packed with flavor, but are lower in fat and simpler to prepare than the original "Scotch eggs" invented by the upmarket London department store Fortnum and Mason.

SERVES: 4	PREP: 25 mins, plus standing & cooling COOK: 30 mins	PER SERVING: 353 cals | 23.2g fat | 7.2g sat fat | 16.2g carbs | 2.2g sugar 1.2g fiber | 18.7g protein | 640mg sodium

INGREDIENTS

4 extra-large eggs
1 tablespoon oil, for oiling
10 ounces sausage links, skins removed
1 tablespoon mild curry paste
1 teaspoon onion seeds
2 tbsp fresh flat-leaf parsley leaves, coarsely chopped
1 cup fresh white bread crumbs
2 tablespoons milk
mango chutney, to serve (optional)

1. Put the eggs into a saucepan and cover with cold water. Bring to a boil, then remove from the heat. Cover the pan and let stand for 6 minutes. Drain and cool under cold running water, then carefully peel off the shells.

2. Preheat the oven to 375°F. Lightly oil a baking pan or line with nonstick parchment paper. Put the sausagemeat, curry paste, onion seeds, and parsley into a bowl. Mix well. Add the bread crumbs and milk and mix again. Divide into four equal portions.

3. Lay a piece of plastic wrap on the work surface. Place one-quarter of the sausage mixture on top and flatten with clean hands to a diameter of about 5 inches. Place an egg in the center and use the plastic wrap to lift and mold the mixture around it. Smooth over the edges to seal. Place on the baking tray. Repeat with the remaining sausage mixture and eggs.

4. Bake in the preheated oven for 25 minutes, until lightly browned. Serve hot or cold with the mango chutney, if desired.

TRY SOMETHING DIFFERENT
To make low-fat sausage-coated eggs closer to the original recipe, omit the spices at step 2 and roll the sausage-covered eggs in ½ cup dried bread crumbs to coat. Place on a baking pan and drizzle each one with 1 teaspoon of olive oil, or spray with cooking spray before baking.

Perfect Pickled Eggs

You can enjoy these as a quick snack with French fries or a glass of beer. Or try serving them as an accompaniment to deli meats and cheeses or chopped and sprinkled over broiled fish such as tuna steaks or sardines.

SERVES: 12	PREP: *15 mins, plus standing* COOK: *20 mins*	PER EGG: *73 cals* | *4.8g fat* | *1.6g sat fat* | *0.7g carbs* | *0.5g sugar* *0g fiber* | *6.3g protein* | *120mg sodium*

INGREDIENTS

12 eggs

1 cup distilled white vinegar

1 cup water

1 tablespoon sugar

2 teaspoons pickling spice

1 teaspoon cumin seeds

2 garlic cloves, peeled and crushed

1 teaspoon salt

12–14 pickled chiles, plus ½ cup of the juice from the jar

1. Put the eggs into a saucepan and cover with cold water. Bring to a boil, then remove from the heat. Cover the pan and let stand for 10 minutes. Drain and cool under cold running water, then peel off the shells.

2. Put the vinegar, water, sugar, pickling spice, cumin, garlic, and salt into a small saucepan. Bring to a boil, then reduce the heat, cover, and simmer for 10 minutes.

3. Layer the eggs and chiles in a sterilized 1-quart jar. Pour in the juice from the chile jar, and add the hot liquid and spices from the pan. Cover the jar and let cool until completely cold.

4. Store in the refrigerator and let stand for at least 3 days before eating. Use within 1 month.

HELPFUL HINT

Make your own pickling spice by mixing together ½ teaspoon each of coriander seeds, mustard seeds, and black peppercorns with 3 allspice berries, 4 cloves, and ¼ teaspoon of ground ginger.

Lunch

BEET & EGG SOUP 44

LENTIL & EGG SALAD 46

SPICY STUFFED SWEET POTATOES 49

CRANBERRY BEAN, TOMATO & EGG SALAD 50

EGGS BAKED IN AVOCADOS 53

THE BENEFITS OF EATING FREE-RANGE EGGS 55

CHICKEN & EGG ROLLS 56

ASPARAGUS & EGG PASTRIES 59

STEAMED GOOSE EGGS WITH FAVA BEANS 60

CROQUE MADAME 63

SALMON & DILL EGG WHITE QUICHE 64

SKINNY TURKEY & EGG SANDWICHES 66

EGGY POTATO & CABBAGE CAKES 69

Beet & Egg Soup

Eggs don't have to be enjoyed simply by themselves or in a cake! Try them in a soup and create a sumptuous dish perfect for lunch or as an impressive dinner party course.

SERVES: 6	PREP: *25 mins, plus cooling & chilling* COOK: *25 mins*	PER SERVING: *150 cals │ 4.6g fat │ 1.9g sat fat │ 25.1g carbs │ 20g sugar* *3.1g fiber │ 6.4g protein │ 1040mg sodium*

INGREDIENTS

4⅔ cups peeled and chopped cooked beets
2 lemons, peeled, seeded and chopped
5½ cups vegetable broth
3 extra-large eggs
1½ tablespoons honey, plus 2 tablespoons for
  drizzling
pinch of salt

TO GARNISH (OPTIONAL)

sour cream, chilled
snipped fresh chives

1. Put the beets and lemons into a large saucepan, pour in the broth, and bring to a boil. Reduce the heat and simmer for 20 minutes.

2. Remove the pan from the heat and let cool slightly. Ladle the soup into a food processor, in batches if necessary, and process to a puree. Pass the soup through a strainer into a bowl to remove any membrane or fibers. Let cool completely.

3. Meanwhile, put the eggs, honey, and a pinch of salt into a food processor and process until thoroughly combined. Gradually add the mixture to the soup, stirring constantly.

4. Cover with plastic wrap and chill in the refrigerator for at least 3 hours. To serve, stir the soup and taste and adjust the seasoning, if necessary. Ladle into bowls, drizzle with honey, garnish with the sour cream and snipped chives, if using, and serve immediately.

TRY SOMETHING DIFFERENT
This chilled soup is perfect for a warm summer day.
Serve as an alfresco lunch with a crunchy salad, fresh
cheese, and country bread.

Lentil & Egg Salad

Salads aren't just for enjoying when the weather is hot. This robust, earthy lentil salad can be rustled up quickly after work and, because it is served just-warm, makes a great dish for cooler days.

SERVES:	PREP: *20–25 mins, plus cooling*	PER SERVING: *383 cals*	*16.9g fat*	*3.9g sat fat*	*37.1g carbs*	*1.9g sugar*
4	COOK: *40 mins*	*18g fiber*	*22g protein*	*1040mg sodium*

INGREDIENTS

3½ cups vegetable broth
2 bay leaves
1 cinnamon stick, halved
2 leeks
1 cup green lentils, rinsed and drained
3 tablespoons olive oil
2 garlic cloves, finely chopped
4 eggs
2 tablespoons capers, drained and chopped
3 cups baby spinach
½ cup coarsely chopped fresh flat-leaf
  parsley, to garnish

DRESSING

2 tablespoons red wine vinegar
1 teaspoon Dijon mustard
salt and pepper (optional)

1. Put the broth, bay leaves, and cinnamon into a saucepan and bring just to a boil. Cut a 3-inch piece from the white bottom of one of the leeks and add this and the lentils to the pan. Cover and simmer for 25 minutes, or until the lentils are tender and nearly all of the broth has been absorbed. Top up with a little boiling water during cooking, if needed. Drain the lentils, transfer to a salad bowl, and discard the cooked leek, bay leaves, and cinnamon stick.

2. Meanwhile, thinly slice the rest of the leeks. Heat 1 tablespoon of olive oil in a skillet over medium heat. Add the leeks and the garlic and sauté for 3–4 minutes, stirring, until just beginning to soften. Remove from the heat and let cool.

3. Put the eggs into a saucepan and pour in enough cold water to cover them by ½ inch. Bring to a boil, then reduce the heat and boil for 8 minutes. Drain immediately, cool quickly under cold running water, then peel and cut into quarters.

4. To make the dressing, put the vinegar, remaining 2 tablespoons of oil, and the mustard in a screw-top jar, season to taste with salt and pepper, if using, screw on the lid, and shake well. Drizzle the dressing over the lentils and toss gently together. Top with the sliced leeks, capers, and spinach. Arrange the hard-boiled eggs over the salad, sprinkle with the parsley, and serve warm.

2

4

4

Spicy Stuffed Sweet Potatoes

A comforting lunch or brunch dish ideal for chilly days. Spanish chorizo sausage varies in flavor from smoky to hot and spicy, in which case you may want to omit the extra chile.

SERVES:	PREP: *20 mins, plus cooling*	PER SERVING: *369 cals*	*15.4g fat*	*5.4g sat fat*	*43.4g carbs*	*9.7g sugar*
4	COOK: *1 hr 5 mins–1 hr 15 mins*	*6.6g fiber*	*14.3g protein*	*680mg sodium*

INGREDIENTS

2 large sweet potatoes

1 tablespoon olive oil, plus 1 tablespoon for oiling

1 small onion, chopped

2 ounces chorizo sausage, chopped into small pieces

1 red chile, seeded and finely chopped (optional)

1 garlic clove, crushed

¼ cup shredded sharp cheddar cheese

3 tablespoons coarsely chopped fresh cilantro, plus extra to garnish

4 medium eggs

salt and pepper (optional)

1. Preheat the oven to 400°F. Oil a baking pan. Place the sweet potatoes on the prepared pan and bake in the preheated oven for 50 minutes–1 hour until cooked through in the center. Set aside for 15 minutes, until cool enough to handle.

2. Meanwhile, heat the oil in a skillet and add the onion, chorizo, and chile, if using. Cook over low heat for 7–8 minutes, stirring occasionally, until the onions are tender and beginning to brown. Add the garlic and cook, stirring, for another minute.

3. Slice the potatoes in half lengthwise and scoop most of the flesh from the centers, leaving a layer around the sides so the thin skins do not collapse. Transfer the flesh to a bowl and mash, then stir in the fried onion mixture, cheese, and cilantro.

4. Pile the mashed sweet potatoes back into the skin halves and place on the baking pan. Make a hollow in the top of each one and carefully break in an egg. Season with salt and pepper, if using. Return to the oven for 15 minutes, until the eggs have just set. Sprinkle with cilantro and serve immediately.

TOP TIP

The sweet potato cases can be cooked and filled the evening or morning before you need them, and stored in the fridge. Heat through in the oven for a few minutes before cracking in the eggs.

Cranberry Bean, Tomato & Egg Salad

If you think salads are tasteless and unsatisfying, then think again! Adding hard-boiled eggs provide them with a heartier edge, and this recipe is no exception.

SERVES: 4	PREP: *20–25 mins, plus soaking* COOK: *1 hr 45 mins–2 hrs 15 mins*	PER SERVING: *492 cals* | *26.1g fat* | *4.5g sat fat* | *45.4g carbs* | *3.2g sugar* *16.8g fiber* | *21.9g protein* | *680mg sodium*

INGREDIENTS

1¼ cups dried cranberry beans, soaked in
* cold water for several hours*
2 large garlic cloves, crushed
juice of 2 lemons
⅓ cup extra virgin olive oil
1 teaspoon salt
1 small onion, finely diced
2 tomatoes, seeded and finely diced
⅔ cup chopped fresh flat-leaf parsley leaves
1 teaspoon cumin seeds, crushed
black pepper (optional)

TO GARNISH

4 hard-boiled eggs, quartered
4 lemon wedges
sumac (optional)

1. Drain the beans, rinse well, and put into a large saucepan. Cover with water and bring to a boil. Boil for 10 minutes, then reduce the heat and simmer for 1½–2 hours, or until tender. Top up with boiling water, if necessary.

2. Drain the beans and transfer to a shallow serving dish. Lightly crush some of them with the back of a wooden spoon.

3. Add the garlic, lemon juice, olive oil, and salt while the beans are still warm. Mix gently, then add the onion, tomatoes, and parsley.

4. Add the cumin seeds and some black pepper, if using, and gently toss.

5. Arrange the egg quarters and lemon wedges on top. Sprinkle with a pinch of sumac, if using, and serve.

WHY NOT TRY
If you don't have sumac, try sprinkling with crushed red pepper flakes instead.

Eggs Baked in Avocados

The idea of eating hot avocado might seem strange, but the combination of creamy flesh, salty bacon, and soft-cooked egg is perfect here.

SERVES:	PREP: *20 mins*	PER SERVING: *277 cals*	*23.6g fat*	*5.2g sat fat*	*9.1g carbs*	*0.8g sugar*
4	COOK: *20 mins*	*6.8g fiber*	*10.2g protein*	*320mg sodium*

INGREDIENTS

5 bacon strips
2 large ripe avocados
4 medium eggs
pepper (optional)
hot toast or salsa, to serve (optional)

1. Preheat the oven to 425°F and the broiler to high. Broil the bacon under the preheated broiler for 5–6 minutes, until crispy, then coarsely chop. Or cook the bacon is a skillet before chopping.

2. Halve the avocados and remove the pits. Scoop out enough flesh to make a hole big enough to hold one egg. Place, cut-side up, balanced over the cups of a muffin pan—the cups will prevent them from tilting over.

3. Drop 3–4 pieces of bacon into the bottom of each avocado. Crack an egg into a cup. To make sure the egg doesn't slide out of the avocado when you pour it in, scoop out the yolk with a spoon and drop it into the hole, then whisk the white lightly with a fork to break it up and pour in just enough to fill the hole.

4. Repeat with the remaining eggs and season to taste with pepper, if using. Bake in the preheated oven for 15 minutes, until the whites of the eggs are just set. Sprinkle with the remaining bacon and serve immediately with hot toast, or salsa, if desired.

HELPFUL HINT

To make a salsa, chop the leftover scooped-out avocado and coarsely chop 2 large ripe tomatoes and 1 small red onion. Put them into a food processor with 2 tablespoons of lemon juice, 1 tablespoon of chopped fresh cilantro, and ¼ teaspoon of chili powder. Blend until finely chopped.

The Benefits of Eating Free-Range Eggs

There are several different options when it comes to buying eggs in the supermarket but the overall opinion is that free-range eggs are the best. There are many factors that support this theory and it is not just because this is the most natural way that chickens would live, there are health benefits too.

Chickens are gregarious creatures. In the wild, they would live in a flock with a natural hierarchy or "pecking order." During the day, they would forage for food, scratching and searching, have regular dust baths to replenish the oils in their feathers, and only seek shelter to cluster together at night in trees or under cover for roosting.

The best eggs come from chickens that are allowed to pasture and roam freely and eat a diet of plants and insects. According to U.S. regulations, the term "free range" can be used if chickens have access to the outdoors, but regulations don't specify how much space or for how long and don't apply to eggs. The American Pastured Poultry Producers' Association (APPPA) promotes raising poultry, including laying chickens, on green pastures, so—unlike factory-reared chickens, which are confined indoors and to a diet of grain and soy—they spend much time outdoors foraging in fresh pasture.

Unsurprisingly, chickens that spend part or all their days foraging in the outdoors are happier and healthier than those kept indoors, so choosing free-range eggs from a reliable supplier when possible is sensible.

Eggs that have been certified organic come from chickens who have "access" to the outdoors and are managed organically. Farmers are not allowed to give them antibiotics or growth hormones and must supply them with organic feed.

The chickens' access to more grass and plants is reflected in the eggs themselves. In general, the yolks from free-range chickens are more golden in color (but this can also be influenced by their feed), which adds a wonderful rich color to cakes and sauces.

In general, free-range eggs have higher levels of omega 3, vitamins A, E, and D and lower levels of total fat, saturated fat and cholesterol and omega 6. Interestingly, vitamin D, which is commonly deficient in many people, can be obtained only from direct sunlight on the skin or from a small list of foods. Eggs are also a really good source of vitamin D.

So, for the best taste, appearance, and health benefits—as well as higher welfare for the hens—it has to be free-range, or organic, eggs every time.

Chicken & Egg Rolls

Delicious straight from the pan or cold at work, the range of flavors here will satisfy your hunger. You'll need metal skewers for this recipe to cook the chicken under the broiler.

SERVES:	PREP: *40 mins, plus marinating & resting*	PER SERVING: *304 cals* | *10.5g fat* | *2.6g sat fat* | *29.2g carbs* | *1.5g sugar*
6	COOK: *25–30 mins*	*1.4g fiber* | *21.9g protein* | *880mg sodium*

INGREDIENTS

2 skinless, boneless chicken breasts, cut into bite-size pieces
1⅔ cups all-purpose flour, plus 1 tablespoon for dusting
1 teaspoon salt
1 tablespoon vegetable or peanut oil
½ cup milk
4 eggs
fresh mint leaves and sliced red onion, to serve (optional)

MARINADE

2 garlic cloves, crushed
1 teaspoon grated fresh ginger
2 teaspoons ground cumin
1 teaspoon chili powder
¼ teaspoon ground turmeric
¼ teaspoon garam masala
2 teaspoons tomato paste
2 tablespoons plain yogurt
1 tablespoon lemon juice
1 teaspoon salt
1 tablespoon vegetable or peanut oil

1. Put all the marinade ingredients into a nonmetallic bowl with the chicken and stir to mix well. Cover and chill in the refrigerator for 6–8 hours, or overnight if possible.

2. When ready to cook, preheat the broiler to medium–high. Thread the marinated chicken onto metal skewers. Place the chicken skewers on a broiler rack and cook under the preheated broiler, turning once, for 12–15 minutes, until cooked through and tender. Remove the chicken from the skewers and keep warm.

3. Meanwhile, sift the flour and salt into a large bowl. Add the oil, milk, and one of the eggs and knead for 8–10 minutes, until smooth. Form into a ball, cover, and let rest for 15–20 minutes.

4. Divide the dough into six equal pieces and form each into a ball. On a lightly floured surface, roll each ball into a 6¼–6½-inch diameter circle, about ⅛ inch thick. Lightly beat the remaining eggs.

5. Heat a nonstick skillet over medium heat. One at a time, put a dough circle into the pan and cook for 1 minute. Flip it over and spread 1 tablespoon of the beaten egg all over the surface. Immediately flip it over again and cook for 30–40 seconds, then remove from the heat. Repeat with all the dough circles.

6. Divide the chicken among the egg rolls and sprinkle with a few mint leaves and some sliced red onion, if desired. Roll tightly to enclose the filling and serve.

Asparagus & Egg Pastries

Spicy smoked paprika is the perfect complement to these baked eggs in puff pastry.

SERVES:	PREP: *20 mins, plus chilling*	PER SERVING: *613 cals*	*36.1g fat*	*16.8g sat fat*	*54.2g carbs*	*5.9g sugar*
4	COOK: *25–30 mins*	*5.1g fiber*	*16.5g protein*	*680mg sodium*

INGREDIENTS

1 (1-pound) package store-bought puff
pastry, thawed if frozen
2 tablespoons flour, for dusting
2 tablespoons milk, for brushing
24 thin asparagus spears (about 10 ounces)
¾ cup store-bought tomato sauce
1 teaspoon hot smoked paprika
4 eggs
salt and pepper (optional)

1. Roll out the pastry on a lightly floured surface to a 14 x 8-inch rectangle, then cut into four pieces to make four 8 x 3½-inch rectangles.

2. Line a baking sheet with nonstick parchment paper and place the pastry rectangles on the sheet. Prick all over with a fork and brush lightly with milk. Chill for 20 minutes.

3. Snap the woody ends off the asparagus and discard. Bring a saucepan of lightly salted water to a boil, then add the asparagus, bring back to a boil and cook for 2–3 minutes, until almost tender. Drain and refresh in cold water, then drain again.

4. Meanwhile, preheat the oven to 400°F. Mix the tomato sauce and paprika together and divide among the pastry crusts, spreading it out almost to the edges. Bake in the preheated oven for 10–12 minutes, until the pastry is puffed around the edges and pale golden.

5. Remove from the oven and top with the asparagus, leaving space for the egg in the middle of each pastry. Crack one egg into a cup and slide into the space created in one of the pastries. Repeat with the remaining eggs, then return the pastries to the oven for 8 minutes, or until the eggs are just set. Season to taste with salt and pepper, if using, and serve immediately.

Steamed Goose Eggs with Fava beans

A dish for spring, when goose eggs are in season, and homegrown beans and herbs are at their best.

SERVES:	PREP: *20–25 mins*
2	COOK: *25 mins*

PER SERVING: *552 cals | 42g fat | 11.8g sat fat | 8.5g carbs | 2.1g sugar 3.4g fiber | 32.6g protein | 1080mg sodium*

INGREDIENTS

⅔ cup fresh or frozen fava beans

3 ounces smoked bacon, diced

4 teaspoons olive oil

2 goose eggs

1 cup chicken broth or vegetable broth

¼ cup torn fresh basil leaves

2 teaspoons lemon juice

2 teaspoons water

pepper (optional)

1. Bring a saucepan of water to a boil, add the beans, and cook for 3 minutes. Drain and rinse under cold running water. Pop the beans out of their skins and discard the skins. Put the bacon into a nonstick skillet with 1 teaspoon of the oil. Cook over high heat until the fat runs off, then cook for 2 minutes, until lightly browned. Remove from the heat, then stir in the beans.

2. Lightly whisk the eggs and broth together with a fork and season to taste with pepper, if using. Stir in half the basil. Pour half the mixture into a 3½-cup heatproof dish, such as a small pie plate, and sprinkle with one-third of the beans and bacon.

3. Place the dish on a piece of scrunched aluminum foil in a deep skillet, so that the dish is raised at least 1 inch from the bottom. Pour in boiling water up to the bottom of the dish, cover the pan with a lid, and steam for 5 minutes, until the eggs are almost set in the middle.

4. Remove the dish from the pan. Pour in the remaining egg mixture and sprinkle with half the remaining bacon and beans. Carefully cover the top of the dish with plastic wrap and steam for an additional 10 minutes, until just set and slightly wobbly in the middle.

5. Sprinkle the steamed eggs with the remaining bacon, beans, and basil. Season to taste with pepper, if using. Whisk the remaining oil with lemon juice and water and drizzle over the top. Serve immediately.

Croque Madame

Baking the sandwiches works as well as grilling or broiling, and if you're making more than two of these French-inspired sandwiches, this method is much easier to manage. Top with a fried egg, if you prefer.

SERVES:	PREP: *15 mins*
4	COOK: *10–12 mins*

PER SERVING: *619 cals | 33.9g fat | 11.9g sat fat | 38.5g carbs | 4.9g sugar 6.1g fiber | 36.6g protein | 1440mg sodium*

INGREDIENTS

8 slices multigrain bread
3 tablespoons butter or reduced-fat spread
1¼ cups shredded Gruyère or Swiss cheese
6 ounces sliced cooked ham
1 teaspoon white wine vinegar
4 extra-large chicken eggs or 4 duck eggs
salt and pepper (optional)
arugula and red onion salad, to serve

1. Preheat the oven to 450°F. Spread the bread with butter and put four slices onto a baking sheet, buttered side down. Top with half the cheese, followed by the ham and the remaining cheese. Cover with the remaining slices of bread, buttered side up.

2. Bake the sandwiches in the preheated oven for 10–12 minutes, until golden brown and the cheese has melted, flipping them over, using a spatula, about halfway through.

3. Meanwhile fill a wide saucepan halfway with water. Add the vinegar and heat until barely simmering. Crack an egg into a cup and slide it into the water. Repeat with the remaining eggs and poach for 2–3 minutes, until the whites are set and the yolks are still soft.

4. Remove from the pan with a slotted spoon and drain on absorbent paper towels. Top each sandwich with an egg and season to taste with salt and pepper, if using. Serve immediately with arugula and red onion salad.

WHY NOT TRY

To make an arugula salad, simply whisk together 2 tablespoons of olive oil, 1 tablespoon of lemon juice, 1 tablespoon of cold water, and some seasoning in a small bowl. Pour it over 1½ cups arugula and 1 small, thinly sliced red onion. Toss together.

Salmon & Dill Egg White Quiche

The dill perfectly complements the salmon in this tempting quiche, ideal as a light dinner on a summer's evening.

| SERVES: | PREP: *20 mins* | | PER SERVING: *156 cals* | *7.8g fat* | *2.3g sat fat* | *4.5g carbs* | *3.7g sugars* |
| 6 | COOK: *50 mins, plus standing* | | *0.8g fiber* | *16.5g protein* | *360mg sodium* |

INGREDIENTS

10 ounces skinless salmon fillet
2 zucchini, thinly sliced
7 egg whites
1 cup milk
2 scallions, thinly sliced
1 tablespoon chopped fresh dill
3 tablespoons freshly grated Parmesan cheese
salt and pepper (optional)
2 tablespoons chopped fresh dill, to garnish (optional)

1. Bring a wide saucepan of water to a boil. Reduce to a gentle simmer, then add the salmon and poach for 6–8 minutes, depending on the thickness of the fish, until just cooked through and the flesh flakes in the center. Drain and flake into chunky pieces.

2. Meanwhile, preheat a dry ridged grill pan, add the zucchini, and cook for about 8 minutes, turning once until cooked through and lightly charred on both sides.

3. Preheat the oven to 350°F. Line an 8–9-inch round baking dish with a piece of nonstick parchment paper large enough to come up the sides. Gently whisk together the egg whites, milk, and scallions in a large, grease-free bowl.

4. Cover the prepared baking dish with half the salmon and zucchini slices and season to taste with salt and pepper, if using. Sprinkle with half the dill and pour over half the egg mixture.

5. Repeat the layers, then sprinkle the top evenly with Parmesan cheese. Bake in the preheated oven for 35–40 minutes, until lightly browned and just set in the middle. Let stand for 15 minutes before lifting from the dish, using the paper. Lightly broil the top if you prefer a browner finish. Serve warm or cold, garnished with chopped fresh dill, if using.

Skinny Turkey & Egg Sandwiches

This sandwich, made with healthy turkey, whole-grain bread, and low-fat cheese, looks and tastes so great you will forget it's low fat! Enjoy with lots of peppery arugula leaves.

SERVES:	PREP: *20 mins*
2	COOK: *10–14 mins*

PER SERVING: *475 cals | 10.3g fat | 3.2g sat fat | 59.3g carbs | 8.9g sugar 7.8g fiber | 37.7g protein | 840mg sodium*

INGREDIENTS

½ red onion, peeled and sliced into whole rings
2 thin turkey cutlets or scallops (3¼–3½ oz each)
½ teaspoon all-purpose seasoning
¼ teaspoon smoked paprika
4 thick slices whole-grain bread
¼ cup low-fat cream cheese
2 hard-boiled eggs, whites only, chopped
2 tomatoes, thinly sliced
1 lemon wedge
½ cup arugula or other peppery greens
salt and pepper (optional)

1. Preheat a ridged grill pan until smoking hot. Add the onion rings and cook for 2–3 minutes on each side until soft and lightly charred. Transfer to a plate.

2. Wipe the turkey with paper towels. Sprinkle with the all-purpose seasoning and paprika and rub into the meat. Arrange on the pan and cook for 3 minutes without moving them, until lightly charred underneath. Turn and cook for 2–3 minutes on the other side, until thoroughly cooked through.

3. Spread the bread with the cream cheese. Cover two slices with the chopped egg white and tomato slices. Cut the turkey in half, arrange on top, and squeeze with a little lemon juice.

4. Divide the arugula between the sandwiches and season to taste with salt and pepper, if using. Top with the remaining bread, cut in half, and serve immediately.

TRY SOMETHING DIFFERENT
The turkey and vegetables shouldn't stick to the grill pan, but they should look lightly charred and be sealed underneath before turning. For the best results, don't be tempted to lift or move them around in the pan until they are ready to turn.

1

2

4

Eggy Potato & Cabbage Cakes

These cakes are a great way of using up leftover vegetables—and "hiding" ones that children wouldn't otherwise try. Try serving them as a side to frankfurters, ham, or smoked fish dishes.

MAKES: 8	PREP: *25 mins, plus cooling*	PER CAKE: *115 cals │ 6.3g fat │ 1.6g sat fat │ 8.8g carbs │ 2.1g sugar*
	COOK: *46–53 mins*	*1.5g fiber │ 6g protein │ 240mg sodium*

INGREDIENTS

1 russet potato, peeled and cut into chunks
5 extra-large eggs
1 tablespoon olive oil, plus extra for frying
1 small onion, peeled and chopped
1 garlic clove, peeled and crushed
1⅔ cups coarsely chopped, cooked cabbage, Brussels sprouts, or parsnip
1 teaspoon English mustard
⅓ cup fine dry bread crumbs
salt and pepper (optional)
ketchup, to serve (optional)

1. Put the potato chunks into a saucepan and cover with water, bring to a boil, then reduce the heat and simmer for 20–25 minutes, until tender. Drain and stir over the heat for 30–60 seconds, then mash.

2. Meanwhile, put four of the eggs into a saucepan, cover with water, and bring to a boil. Simmer for 7 minutes, drain, then cool under cold running water. Peel and coarsely chop the eggs.

3. Heat the oil in a large nonstick skillet. Add the onion and gently sauté for 3–4 minutes, until soft, then stir in the garlic and add the cooked vegetables. Spread out over the bottom of the pan and cook for another 3–4 minutes without stirring, until brown underneath. Remove from the heat.

4. Transfer to a large bowl. Add the potato and egg. Season to taste with salt and pepper, if using. Beat the remaining egg with the mustard, add to the bowl, and mix well. Divide the mixture into eight equal portions and shape each portion into a 3¼-inch round patty.

5. Place the bread crumbs on a plate. Press the patties into them to cover both sides. Wipe out the skillet. Add 1 teaspoon of oil and heat. Add four patties and cook for about 3 minutes, until golden brown underneath. Turn, add another teaspoon of oil, and cook for an additional 3 minutes. Remove from the pan and keep warm while cooking the remaining patties in the same way. Serve immediately with ketchup.

TOP TIP
Add just enough oil to brown the patties. Doing so prevents the eggs from soaking up too much oil and possibly exploding when placed over high heat.

Mains

BARLEY & ASPARAGUS RISOTTO WITH POACHED EGG 73

ZUCCHINI FRITTERS WITH POACHED EGGS 74

SPINACH, PEA & FETA WHOLE-WHEAT TART 77

ARTICHOKE & RED PEPPER TORTILLA 78

HAM & EGG PIE 81

HOW TO BUY THE BEST EGGS & KEEP THEM FRESH 83

FIORENTINA PIZZA 84

EGG-TOPPED HAMBURGERS 86

TOMATO & CARAMELIZED ONION STRATA 89

EGG & LENTIL CURRY 90

SKINNY CARBONARA 93

MEATLOAF STUFFED WITH QUAIL EGGS 94

STEAK TARTARE 97

EGG, MEATBALL & TOMATO STEW 98

Barley & Asparagus Risotto with Poached Egg

A dish to make in spring when goose eggs and asparagus are both in season. Humble pearl barley makes a creamy and delicious risotto. It takes longer to cook than risotto rice but requires much less stirring.

SERVES:	PREP: *20–25 mins*
6	COOK: *1 hr 30 mins*

PER SERVING: *529 Cals | 25.3g fat | 8.8g sat fat | 47.8g carbs | 5.1g sugar 9.4g fiber | 27g protein | 800mg sodium*

INGREDIENTS

2 tablespoons butter
1 large onion, peeled and finely chopped
1 celery stalk, finely chopped
2 garlic cloves, crushed
2 chicken bouillon cubes
6⅓ cups boiling water
1½ cups pearl barley
⅔ cup hard dry cider or apple juice
16 asparagus spears, trimmed
1 teaspoon white wine vinegar
6 goose (or duck) eggs
3 tablespoons low-fat cream cheese
1⅓ cups freshly grated Parmesan cheese
pepper (optional)

1. Heat the butter in a large saucepan until melted and foaming. Add the onion, celery, and garlic. Cover and cook over low heat for 10 minutes, until the onion looks translucent. Meanwhile, dissolve the bouillon cubes in 3½ cups of the boiling water.

2. Add the barley to the pan and stir to coat in the buttery juices. Pour in the cider or juice and boil rapidly until most of the liquid has evaporated. Pour in the broth and simmer for 1 hour, stirring occasionally and adding the remaining boiling water, as necessary, after 30 minutes.

3. Meanwhile, steam the asparagus for 3–4 minutes, or until tender. Lift out with a slotted spoon and refresh in iced water, then drain and chop.

4. When the risotto is almost cooked, fill a wide saucepan halfway with water, add the vinegar, and heat until simmering. Crack the eggs, one at a time, into a cup, then slide them into the water. Poach for 9 minutes, until the whites are just set. Lift out with a slotted spoon and drain on absorbent paper towels.

5. Stir the cream cheese into the risotto until melted. Season to taste with pepper, if using. Add the asparagus and heat through for 1 minute, then stir in half the Parmesan cheese.

6. To serve, ladle the risotto into warm bowls and top with the poached eggs. Season to taste with pepper, if using, and sprinkle with the remaining Parmesan cheese.

Zucchini Fritters with Poached Eggs

Pairing zucchini fritters with a poached egg is a perfect idea for a quick, nourishing dinner after a long day, and the caramelized onions offer a subtle sweetness!

SERVES:	PREP: *25 mins, plus cooling*	PER SERVING: *564 cals*	*28.8g fat*	*5.4g sat fat*	*59.6g carbs*	*14.9g sugar*
4	COOK: *1 hr*	*4.7g fiber*	*17g protein*	*720mg sodium*

INGREDIENTS

2 tablespoons extra virgin olive oil

5 red onions, sliced

1 tablespoon brown sugar

1⅔ cups all-purpose flour

1½ teaspoons baking powder

1 egg, lightly beaten, plus 4 eggs for poaching or frying

1 cup milk

2 zucchini, shredded

1 cup sunflower oil

salt and pepper (optional)

1. Heat the olive oil in a large, heavy saucepan over medium heat, add the onions, and sauté for 5 minutes, or until softened. Stir in the sugar and reduce the heat, cover, and cook for 30 minutes, or until the onions are deep brown, stirring occasionally. Season to taste with salt and pepper, if using, and let cool.

2. To make the fritters, mix the flour and baking powder in a large bowl, then make a well in the center. Whisk the beaten egg and milk together, then use a wooden spoon to incorporate into the flour. Season to taste with salt and pepper, if using, and stir in the shredded zucchini.

3. Heat the sunflower oil in a wide, deep pan and drop in tablespoons of the batter. Cook, in batches, if necessary, until golden brown on both sides, turning once. Drain on paper towels and keep warm.

4. Meanwhile poach the eggs. Bring a shallow pan of water to a gentle simmer. Crack an egg into a small bowl or ramekin, then slide the egg into the water as close to the water as possible. Using a large spoon, gently fold any stray strands of white around the yolk and cook to your liking. Repeat with the other eggs.

5. To serve, put three fritters onto each individual plate, place an egg on top, and spoon some of the caramelized onions over the fritters. Serve immediately.

Spinach, Pea & Feta Whole Wheat-Tart

Whole-wheat flour, spinach, and peas offer great health benefits for the body and, by marrying them together with an egg mixture, you can experience the taste benefits too!

SERVES:	PREP: *35 mins, plus chilling & cooling*
6	COOK: *50 mins–1 hr 5 mins*

PER SERVING: *439 cals | 27.1g fat | 15.6g sat fat | 35.9g carbs | 4.9g sugar 6.2g fiber | 16.4g protein | 280mg sodium*

INGREDIENTS

½ tablespoon unsalted butter
3 scallions, thinly sliced
7 cups baby spinach
⅔ cup shelled peas
3 eggs
1 cup milk
⅔ cup drained and finely crumbled feta cheese
6 cherry tomatoes, halved
sea salt and pepper (optional)

PASTRY DOUGH

1 stick unsalted butter, cut into cubes
1¾ cups whole-wheat flour, plus 1 tablespoon to dust
2 eggs, beaten
salt and pepper (optional)

1. To make the dough, put the butter and flour into a mixing bowl and season to taste with salt and pepper, if using. Rub the butter into the flour until it resembles fine bread crumbs. Gradually mix in enough egg to make a soft but not sticky dough.

2. Lightly dust a work surface with whole-wheat flour. Knead the dough gently, then roll it out on the work surface to a little larger than a 10-inch loose-bottom tart pan. Lift the dough over the rolling pin, ease it into the pan, and press it into the sides. Trim the dough so that it stands a little above the top of the pan to allow for shrinkage, then prick the bottom with a fork.

3. Cover the tart shell with plastic wrap and chill in the refrigerator for 15–30 minutes. Meanwhile, preheat the oven to 375°F.

4. To make the filling, melt the butter in a skillet over medium heat. Add the scallions and cook for 2–3 minutes, or until softened. Add the spinach, turn the heat to high, and cook, stirring, until wilted. Set aside to cool.

5. Cook the peas in a small saucepan of boiling water for 2 minutes. Drain, then plunge into iced water and drain again. Crack the eggs into a bowl, add the milk, season to taste with salt and pepper, if using, and beat with a fork.

6. Remove the plastic wrap from the tart shell and line with parchment paper, add pie weights or dried beans, and put onto a baking sheet. Bake for 10 minutes, then remove the paper and weights and bake for an additional 5 minutes, or until the bottom of the tart is crisp and dry.

7. Drain any cooking juices from the scallions and spinach into the eggs. Transfer the onion mixture to the tart shell, add the peas, then sprinkle with the cheese. Fork the eggs and milk together once more, then pour into the tart shell and dot the tomatoes over the top. Bake for 40–50 minutes, or until set and golden. Let cool for 20 minutes, then serve.

Artichoke & Red Pepper Tortilla

Traditionally Spanish in origin, this egg-based dish allows you to utilize your culinary flair. Follow the recipe exactly or use it as a guide to create a tortilla, delicious by itself or as a side dish.

SERVES:	PREP: *25 mins*	PER SERVING: *262 cals* │ *21.6g fat* │ *3.9g sat fat* │ *5.6g carbs* │ *2.4g sugar*
8	COOK: *20–25 mins*	*2.9g fiber* │ *9.9g protein* │ *360mg sodium*

INGREDIENTS

1 large onion, thinly sliced
9 extra-large eggs
12 artichoke hearts in oil, drained and
  quartered, plus 2 tablespoons oil reserved
1 cup drained and chopped, roasted
  red peppers in oil, plus 2 tablespoons oil
  reserved
3 tablespoons olive oil, for frying
salt and pepper (optional)

1. Heat the reserved oil from the artichokes and roasted peppers in a 10-inch skillet over high heat. Reduce the heat, add the onion, and sauté, stirring, for 8–10 minutes, until golden.

2. Beat the eggs in a large bowl. Stir in the artichoke hearts and roasted red peppers and season to taste with salt and pepper, if using.

3. Using a slotted spoon, transfer the onions to the bowl, leaving as much oil in the pan as possible.

4. Add 2–3 tablespoons of olive oil to the pan to make it up to 4 tablespoons. Heat over high heat, swirling so it coats the side of the pan.

5. Add the egg mixture and smooth the surface. Cook for 30 seconds, then reduce the heat to medium and cook for another 5–7 minutes, shaking the pan occasionally, until the bottom is set and using a spatula to loosen the sides of the tortilla.

6. Position a large plate over the top of the pan. Invert the pan and plate, holding them together, so the tortilla drops onto the plate.

7. Add 1 tablespoon of olive oil to the pan and heat. Slide the tortilla into the pan, cooked-side up. Continue cooking for 3–5 minutes, until the eggs are set and the bottom is golden brown.

8. Slide the tortilla onto a plate. Cut into wedges and serve hot, warm, or at room temperature.

Ham & Egg Pie

A freshly baked pie is a great source of comfort at the end of a hard day. The ham, egg, and scallions in this recipe work perfectly alongside each other, great for sharing with family and friends.

SERVES: 4	PREP: 25 mins, plus cooling COOK: 50–55 mins

PER SERVING: *603 cals | 33.7g fat | 18.4g sat fat | 52.4g carbs | 2.3g sugar 2.6g fiber | 21.6g protein | 920mg sodium*

INGREDIENTS

4 eggs
6 ounces cooked ham
3 scallions, finely chopped
⅔ cup milk, plus extra for glazing
salt and pepper (optional)

PASTRY DOUGH

2 cups all-purpose flour
1 stick butter
pinch of salt
2 tablespoons cold water, to mix

1. Preheat the oven to 400°F.

2. To make the dough, put the flour into a bowl, rub in the butter until the mixture resembles fine bread crumbs, then season with a pinch of salt and add enough water to make a smooth dough.

3. Bring a small saucepan of water to a boil, add two eggs, and cook for 8 minutes, then cool quickly in cold water.

4. Divide the dough in two, one piece slightly larger than the other, and roll out the larger piece to line an 8-inch tart pan.

5. Peel and chop the hard-boiled eggs and cut the ham into small pieces. Place the eggs, ham, and scallions in the pastry shell.

6. Beat the remaining eggs with the milk, season to taste with salt and pepper, if using, and pour over the ham mixture.

7. Roll out the other piece of dough, dampen the edge of the pastry bottom, and lay the lid on top. Seal well and crimp the edges of the pie. Glaze with a little milk and place the pie on a baking sheet.

8. Bake in the preheated oven for 10 minutes, then reduce the oven temperature to 350°F and bake for an additional 30 minutes, until the pastry is golden. Serve warm or cold.

How To Buy The Best Eggs & Keep Them Fresh

Where you buy your eggs is, of course, a personal choice, whether it's from a neighbor who keeps a few chickens in their backyard, a farm store, or your local supermarket. Just follow these simple rules to keep your eggs in the best condition.

Eggs bought from a store may have a sell-by date on the carton, but it is not required by law. A three-digit number on the carton label is. It indicates the date the eggs were "candled" and graded; 365 would be December 31. Storing eggs in the refrigerator is the safest way, keeping the pointed ends facing down. If you store them outside the refrigerator, keep them at a constant temperature below 68°F.

When storing your eggs, make sure that they are kept away from strong smelling foods and raw meat. Brown eggshells are less porous than white, so brown eggs may keep for longer.

Always wash your hands before and after handling eggs, don't use cracked or dirty eggs, and don't reuse leftover egg dishes. The two chalazae, or threads, running through the egg white are what secure the yolk to the shell. If you have any spots of blood in the yolk or brown spots in the white, simply remove them with a piece of shell, although they are harmless.

The flavor of an egg won't change over time. The flavor difference between a fresh egg and one stored for several weeks in a refrigerator is barely detectable, although the moisture content will change. Because their shells are porous, eggs dehydrate over time. As the egg gets older, the white becomes more watery and the yolk becomes flatter and less spherical. If you need to check the freshness of a raw egg, simply place it in a bowl of cold water. The older the egg, the larger the pocket of air within it. If the egg drops to the bottom of the bowl on its side, it's fresh; however, if it drops more slowly and bounces on the bottom, then it's 2–3 weeks old. An egg that floats on the surface of the water could be several months old and should be discarded.

If you keep your eggs in the refrigerator, always remove them about 30 minutes before they are needed. This will help prevent the shells from cracking if you are cooking the whole egg in hot water, and the egg white will be firmer.

Eggs will normally keep for about 3 weeks (depending on their freshness when purchased). Once removed from their shells, they must be kept covered in the refrigerator. If storing egg yolks on their own, cover with a little cold water to help keep them fresh, but use within 2 days.

Egg whites will keep for up to 2 weeks, or can be frozen for up to 3 months in a sealed container.

Use the freshest eggs you can get for poaching, because they tend to hold their shape best during cooking. Egg whites that are 3–4 days old are better for whisking.

Fiorentina Pizza

Bring Italy to your own kitchen with this tempting pizza recipe, served with an egg in the center for that extra gourmet feel. This recipe makes four 7½-inch/19-cm pizzas.

MAKES:	PREP: *40–45 mins, plus rising*
4 PIZZAS	COOK: *13–18 mins*

PER PIZZA: *608 cals | 27.1g fat | 7.5g sat fat | 61g carbs | 4.4g sugar 4.2g fiber | 28.1g protein | 1320mg sodium*

INGREDIENTS

2¼ cups white bread flour, plus 1 tablespoon extra for dusting

1 teaspoon active dry yeast

1½ teaspoons salt

¾ cup lukewarm water

1 tablespoon olive oil, plus 1 tablespoon for oiling

TOPPING

9 cups spinach, washed and drained

¾ cup prepared pizza sauce

2 garlic cloves, finely chopped

¼ cup pitted and halved black olives

2 tablespoons garlic olive oil

4 eggs

1 cup finely grated Grana Padano cheese

salt and pepper (optional)

1. Sift the flour into a mixing bowl and add the yeast and salt, making a small well in the top. Mix the water and oil together and pour into the bowl, using a blunt knife to gradually combine all the flour to make a sticky dough.

2. Lightly flour the work surface and your hands and knead the dough for about 10 minutes, until smooth and elastic.

3. Cover the dough with some lightly oiled plastic wrap or a damp dish towel and let rise for about an hour, or until it has doubled in size.

4. Punch down the dough and gently knead for about a minute, then divide into four balls. To roll out the dough, flatten each ball, then, using a rolling pin, roll out on a lightly floured work surface, giving a quarter turn between each roll.

5. Preheat the oven to 425°F. Place the pizza crusts on two baking sheets, using a rolling pin to transfer them from the work surface.

6. Wash the spinach and put into a large saucepan with the water clinging to the leaves. Cover and cook for 2–3 minutes, until wilted, then squeeze out the excess water between two plates. Return to the pan.

7. Divide the pizza sauce among the four pizza crusts, spreading almost to the edges. Sprinkle with the garlic, top with the spinach and olives, and drizzle with the garlic oil.

8. Bake in the preheated oven for 8–10 minutes, then remove from the oven and make a small indentation in the center of each pizza. Pour an egg into each indentation, sprinkle with the cheese, and season to taste with salt and pepper, if using.

9. Return to the oven and bake for another 3–5 minutes, or until the eggs are just cooked and the crusts are crisp underneath. Serve immediately.

Egg-topped Hamburgers

Feel free to cook the eggs to your preference, but note that if there is some runny yolk, it makes a wonderful sauce for these burgers.

MAKES:	PREP: *20 mins*	PER BURGER: *551 cals* | *30.6g fat* | *13.7g sat fat* | *30.4g carbs* | *6.6g sugar*
4	COOK: *15 mins*	*1.8g fiber* | *35.8g protein* | *520mg sodium*

INGREDIENTS

1 pound ground chuck beef

2 tablespoons Worcestershire sauce

4 English muffins

4 tablespoons butter

2 teaspoons vegetable oil

4 eggs

½ teaspoon salt

½ teaspoon pepper

1. Combine the beef with half the Worcestershire sauce in a large bowl. Divide the mixture into four equal portions and shape each portion into a patty about ½ inch wider than the muffins, making a dimple in the center of each patty.

2. Halve the muffins and spread each half with butter.

3. Heat a large skillet over medium–high heat. Put the muffin halves into the pan, buttered side down, and cook for about 2 minutes. Put two muffin halves on each of four plates.

4. Add the patties to the pan and cook for about 4 minutes, until brown. Turn and cook on the other side for 4 minutes, or until cooked to your preference. Place a burger on one of the muffin halves on each plate and drizzle with the remaining Worcestershire sauce.

5. Add the oil to the pan, swirling to coat. Add the eggs and sprinkle with the salt and pepper. Cover and cook for about 3 minutes, until the whites are set and the yolks are beginning to set at the edges. Top each burger with an egg and the top half of a muffin. Serve immediately.

TRY SOMETHING DIFFERENT

As well as egg, tomato, bacon, mushrooms, lettuce, or green leaves make a tasty filling to these burgers. You could also try serving the egg on top of the bun.

Tomato & Caramelized Onion Strata

This classic American dish combines a mixture of flavors to form a tasty variation on a traditional casserole. Cold or hot, for one or for a group, it's a great way to use up the eggs in your kitchen.

SERVES:	PREP: *20 mins*
4	COOK: *1 hr 5 mins, plus standing*

PER SERVING: *441 cals | 24.8g fat | 10.6g sat fat | 30g carbs | 9.7g sugar 2.4g fiber | 24.7g protein | 480mg sodium*

INGREDIENTS

4 teaspoons olive oil, plus 1 tablespoon for oiling
1 large onion, chopped
½ teaspoon sugar
1 tablespoon snipped fresh chives
12 cherry tomatoes
½ (10-ounce) loaf day-old French bread, cubed
1¼ cups shredded Gruyère or Swiss cheese
3 extra-large eggs
1½ cups milk
1 teaspoon Dijon mustard
2 teaspoons chopped fresh thyme
pepper (optional)
1 tablespoon snipped fresh chives, to garnish
salad greens and chutney, to serve (optional)

1. Preheat the oven to 400°F. Heat the oil in a skillet. Add the onion and gently sauté for 12–14 minutes, until soft and golden brown. Stir in the sugar and cook, stirring, for 1 minute. Remove from the heat and stir in the chives.

2. Meanwhile, put the tomatoes into a small, lightly oiled roasting pan and roast in the preheated oven for 7–8 minutes, until soft and the skins are beginning to split. Reduce the oven temperature to 350°F.

3. Lightly oil a deep 1-quart ovenproof dish. Sprinkle one-third of the bread cubes in the bottom of the dish, followed by one-third each of the onions, roasted tomatoes, and cheese. Season with pepper, if using. Repeat the layers two times.

4. Put the eggs, milk, mustard, and thyme into a bowl and whisk together with a fork. Slowly pour the mixture over the bread and vegetables in the dish. Bake for 50 minutes, or until just set in the middle. Let stand for 5 minutes, then sprinkle with chives. Serve with salad greens and chutney, if desired.

TOP TIP
The exact cooking time of the strata will depend on the depth of the dish that you've used to cook it in. Once it has set in the middle it is cooked.

Egg & Lentil Curry

Hard-boiled eggs become a great subsidiary to the spiciness of this authentic curry, proving their many capabilities as an incredibly diverse and delicious ingredient once again.

SERVES:	PREP: *20–25 mins*
4	COOK: *45 mins*

PER SERVING: *349 cals | 21.8g fat | 6.9g sat fat | 23.9g carbs | 5.5g sugar 4.1g fiber | 16.7g protein | 520mg sodium*

INGREDIENTS

3 tablespoons ghee or vegetable oil

1 large onion, chopped

2 garlic cloves, chopped

1-inch piece fresh ginger, chopped

½ teaspoon chili powder

1 teaspoon ground coriander

1 teaspoon ground cumin

1 teaspoon paprika

½ cup split red lentils

2 cups vegetable broth

1 cup canned diced tomatoes

6 eggs

¼ cup coconut milk

2 tomatoes, cut into wedges

salt (optional)

sprigs of fresh cilantro, to garnish (optional)

chapatis or other flatbreads, to serve (optional)

1. Heat the ghee in a saucepan, add the onion, and sauté gently for 3 minutes. Stir in the garlic, ginger, and spices and cook gently, stirring frequently, for 1 minute.

2. Stir in the lentils, broth, and tomatoes and bring to a boil. Reduce the heat, cover, and simmer, stirring occasionally, for 30 minutes, until the lentils are tender.

3. Meanwhile, put the eggs into a saucepan of cold water and bring to a boil. Reduce the heat and simmer for 10 minutes. Drain and cover immediately with cold water.

4. Stir the coconut milk into the lentil mixture and season to taste with salt, if using. Process the mixture in a blender or food processor until smooth. Return to the pan and heat through.

5. Shell the hard-boiled eggs and cut into quarters. Divide the hard-boiled egg quarters and tomato wedges among warm serving plates. Spoon the hot lentil sauce over the eggs and garnish with sprigs of cilantro, if using. Serve hot with chapatis, if desired.

1

2

4

Skinny Carbonara

A reduced-fat version of the well-known pasta dish. You can rustle it up in less than half an hour from ingredients you may already have in the kitchen.

SERVES:	PREP: *20 mins*
4	COOK: *18–20 mins*

PER SERVING: *523 cals | 20g fat | 8.4g sat fat | 57.9g carbs | 3.1g sugar 2.6g fiber | 26g protein | 600mg sodium*

INGREDIENTS
12 ounces dried spaghetti
2 extra-large eggs
1 cup freshly grated Parmesan cheese
2 tablespoons chopped fresh flat-leaf parsley
4 ounces pancetta or smoked dry-cure bacon strips, chopped
1 teaspoon olive oil
⅓ cup reduced-fat cream cheese
pepper (optional)

1. Bring a large saucepan of lightly salted water to a boil. Add the spaghetti and cook for 10–12 minutes, or according to package directions, until tender but still firm to the bite.

2. Meanwhile whisk together the eggs, half the Parmesan cheese, and the parsley with a fork. Put the pancetta and oil into a large skillet. Heat gently until the bacon fat starts to run, then cook for 2 minutes, or until lightly browned.

3. Ladle ⅔ cup of hot cooking water from the spaghetti and reserve, then drain the spaghetti. Add the spaghetti water and cream cheese to the bacon pan, then heat, stirring, until melted and smooth. Remove from the heat.

4. Working quickly, add the hot spaghetti to the bacon pan, pour in the egg mixture, and toss everything together—the heat from the pasta and pan will thicken the sauce to a coating consistency. Season to taste with pepper, if using, and divide among warm bowls. Sprinkle with the remaining cheese and serve immediately.

TOP TIP
Try to have everyone sitting at the table ready to eat as this dish is best served straight away; if it stands for a while and starts to look dry stir in some more hot pasta water or a splash of hot water from the kettle.

Meatloaf Stuffed with Quail Eggs

The smaller quails eggs are perfect inside this flavorsome meatloaf recipe for a slightly different take on the classic dish.

SERVES:	PREP: *40 mins, plus cooling*	PER SERVING: *346 cals* | *24g fat* | *8.3g sat fat* | *7g carbs* | *1.3g sugar*
8	COOK: *1 hr 20 mins, plus resting*	*1.3g fiber* | *24.9g protein* | *560mg sodium*

INGREDIENTS

2 tablespoons oil, for oiling
16 quail eggs
10 cups young spinach
½ teaspoon freshly grated nutmeg, or to taste
1 pound ground round beef
1 pound ground pork
6 smoked dry-cure bacon strips, finely chopped
1¼ cups fresh white bread crumbs
1 onion, finely chopped
2 garlic cloves, peeled and crushed
2 teaspoons fresh thyme leaves
2 teaspoons finely chopped fresh rosemary
salt and pepper (optional)

1. Lightly oil a 9 x 5 x 3-inch loaf pan and line the bottom with parchment paper. Bring a saucepan of water to a boil. Add the eggs and cook over low heat for 4 minutes. Scoop out with a slotted spoon and place in a bowl of iced water. When completely cool, carefully peel off the shells.

2. Wash the spinach in cold water, drain, and put into a large saucepan with the water still clinging to the leaves. Cover and cook for 3–4 minutes, until wilted. Drain and refresh under cold running water.

3. Place the spinach between two plates and squeeze out the excess water. Transfer to a bowl. Add the nutmeg, and season to taste with salt and pepper, if using.

4. Preheat the oven to 350°F. Put the beef, pork, bacon, bread crumbs, onion, garlic, thyme, and rosemary into a large bowl. Season to taste with salt and pepper, if using, and mix well.

5. Spread about one-third of the meat mixture over the bottom of the prepared pan, leaving the top uneven. Sprinkle with half the spinach leaves—you will need to pull them apart—and half the eggs, keeping them away from the sides of the pan.

6. Repeat the layers one more time, then cover with the remaining meat mixture. Bake in the preheated oven for 1¼ hours, until the meatloaf has shrunk slightly from the sides of the pan and there are no pink juices running from the center when tested with the tip of a knife.

7. Pour off the excess juices. Let the meatloaf rest for 10 minutes before turning out of the pan. Serve hot or cold.

Steak Tartare

Just as tasty raw as they are fried, scrambled, or poached, an egg yolk looks tempting on top of this gourmet dish and tastes even better!

SERVES: 2	PREP: *20 mins, plus chilling* COOK: *n/a*

PER SERVING: *259 cals | 13g fat | 4.6g sat fat | 3.1g carbs | 1.2g sugar 0.8g fiber | 30.9g protein | 880mg sodium*

INGREDIENTS

9 ounces best-quality filet mignon or tenderloin steak

1 tablespoon finely chopped parsley

1 tablespoon finely chopped capers

1 tablespoon finely chopped shallots

1 tablespoon finely chopped pickles

2 dashes hot sauce

2 dashes Worcestershire sauce

1 tablespoon Dijon mustard

½ teaspoon salt

2 egg yolks (kept separate)

1. Chill all the ingredients, a cutting board, and a mixing bowl for 20 minutes before you begin. Remove from the refrigerator and finely chop the steak.

2. Put the steak into the chilled bowl. Add all the remaining ingredients, except the egg yolks, and mix them into the beef with a fork.

3. Shape the mixture into two round patties and make an indent in the middle of each. Place in the refrigerator until ready to serve.

4. To serve, place each patty in the middle of a plate and lay a raw egg yolk in the indent.

HELPFUL HINT

Select fine, well-aged steak for this dish and be sure you chop by hand—not mechanically with a mixer—or it will become overprocessed and tough.

Egg, Meatball & Tomato Stew

Put your own twist on this traditional Moroccan stew with meatballs, tomatoes and, of course, eggs to bring something a little different to this timeless dish.

SERVES:	PREP: *25–30 mins*	PER SERVING: *564 cals* | *42.1g fat* | *15.3g sat fat* | *15g carbs* | *9.2g sugar*
4	COOK: *37–47 mins*	*2.8g fiber* | *30.4g protein* | *720mg sodium*

INGREDIENTS

*1 pound lean fresh ground lamb or fresh
   ground round beef*
2 tablespoons finely chopped fresh parsley
1 teaspoon cumin seeds, crushed
1 teaspoon ground cinnamon
½ teaspoon paprika
2 tablespoons olive oil
salt and pepper (optional)

SAUCE

1 large onion, finely chopped
2 garlic cloves, peeled and crushed
1½ teaspoons cumin seeds, crushed
1 teaspoon paprika
1 (28-ounce) can diced tomatoes
½ teaspoon crushed red pepper flakes
4 eggs
salt and pepper (optional)
*2–3 tablespoons chopped fresh cilantro, to
   garnish*

1. To make the meatballs, put the meat, parsley, cumin seeds, cinnamon, and paprika into a bowl, season to taste with salt and pepper, if using, and mix well together. Roll into 24 walnut-size balls.

2. Preheat the oven to 400°F. Heat the oil in a large skillet and cook the meatballs for 2–3 minutes, in batches if necessary, until brown all over. Transfer to a plate with a slotted spoon.

3. To make the sauce, add the onion to the pan and sauté gently for 10 minutes, until soft and golden brown. Add the garlic, cumin seeds, and paprika and heat, stirring, for a few seconds, then stir in the tomatoes and red pepper flakes. Simmer for 7–10 minutes, until the sauce is reduced and thick. Season to taste with salt and pepper, if using, and remove from the heat.

4. Add the meatballs to the pan. Stir, being careful not to break them up, then transfer to an ovenproof dish. Make four shallow dips in the sauce and carefully break an egg into each one. Bake in the preheated oven for 15–20 minutes, until the eggs are just set. Sprinkle with cilantro and serve immediately.

TOP TIP
You will need to add a little extra oil to the pan in step 3 if the ground meat you've used was very lean.

Desserts

BAKED PASSION FRUIT CUSTARDS 102

CHOCOLATE MOUSSE 105

CARDAMOM WAFFLES WITH BLACKBERRIES & FIGS 106

CRÈME CARAMEL 109

APRICOT & ROSEMARY CLAFOUTIS 110

ESSENTIAL EQUIPMENT 112

CRÈME BRÛLÉE 115

CLASSIC MERINGUES 117

TIRAMISU 118

BAKED LEMON CHEESECAKE 121

LEMON ANGEL FOOD CAKE 123

GOAN LAYERED COCONUT CAKE 124

RASPBERRY & MASCARPONE ICE CREAM 127

Baked Passion Fruit Custards

A tropical treat combining passion fruit pulp with creamy coconut milk and orange flower water to create a delightful dessert.

| SERVES: | PREP: *20 mins* | | PER SERVING: *247 cals* | *15.4g fat* | *10.2g sat fat* | *19.6g carbs* | *17.1g sugar* |
| 4 | COOK: *40–45 mins* | | *1.9g fiber* | *9.2g protein* | *80mg sodium* | | |

INGREDIENTS

4 passion fruit
4 extra-large eggs
¾ cup coconut milk
¼ cup sugar
1 teaspoon orange flower water

1. Preheat the oven to 350°F. Halve three passion fruit, scoop out the flesh, and rub through a strainer to remove the seeds.

2. Beat together the eggs, passion fruit juice, coconut milk, sugar, and orange flower water until smooth.

3. Pour the custard into four 1-cup ovenproof dishes, place in a baking pan, and pour in hot water to reach halfway up the dishes.

4. Bake in the oven for 40–45 minutes or until just set. Scoop the pulp from the remaining passion fruit and spoon a little onto each dish to serve. Serve the custards slightly warm.

WHY NOT TRY

These passion fruit custards are equally delicious served chilled. For a dinner party, make a batch in the morning and chill in the refrigerator until required.

Chocolate Mousse

For a luxurious treat, combine chocolate and eggs to create the perfect mousse for a sweet, indulgent fix after dinner.

SERVES: 6	PREP: *20 mins, plus cooling & chilling* COOK: *6–8 mins*

PER SERVING: *392 cals | 26.8g fat | 14.7g sat fat | 28.6g carbs | 20g sugar 4.3g fiber | 7.5g protein | 40mg sodium*

INGREDIENTS

10 ounces semisweet chocolate, broken into small pieces, plus 1 ounce finely chopped, to serve
1½ tablespoons unsalted butter
1 tablespoon brandy
4 eggs, separated

1. Put the broken chocolate pieces into a heatproof bowl set over a saucepan of gently simmering water. Add the butter and melt with the chocolate, stirring, until smooth. Remove from the heat, stir in the brandy, and let cool slightly. Add the egg yolks and beat until smooth.

2. In a separate bowl, whisk the egg whites until stiff peaks have formed, then fold into the chocolate mixture. Spoon into small dessert dishes or cups and level the surfaces. Transfer to the refrigerator and chill for at least 4 hours, or until set.

3. Take the mousse out of the refrigerator and serve immediately, sprinkled with finely chopped chocolate pieces.

HELPFUL HINT
When melting the chocolate, be sure the bottom of the bowl doesn't touch the water, otherwise the chocolate can burn and be ruined.

Cardamom Waffles with Blackberries & Figs

Aromatic cardamom adds a wonderful depth of flavor to these fabulous fruit-topped waffles, so dig out your waffle maker and cook up this satisfying weekend family breakfast when late-summer blackberries are at their best.

SERVES:	PREP: *25 mins, plus resting*
6	COOK: *10–17 mins*

PER SERVING: *422 cals | 17.3g fat | 7.8g sat fat | 53.9g carbs | 23.7g sugar 7.3g fiber | 16.1g protein | 200mg sodium*

INGREDIENTS

5 extra-large eggs, divided

pinch of salt

1 teaspoon ground cardamom

3½ tablespoons unsalted butter, melted and cooled

1 cup low-fat milk

1¾ cups plus 2 tablespoons whole-wheat flour

1 tablespoon olive oil, for brushing

⅔ cup Greek-style plain yogurt

6 ripe figs, quartered

1⅓ cups blackberries

⅓ cup agave syrup, to serve

1. Put the egg yolks, salt, and cardamom into a bowl and beat well with a wooden spoon. Stir in the melted butter. Slowly beat in the milk until completely incorporated. Gradually add the flour until you have a thick batter.

2. In a separate bowl, whisk the egg whites until they form stiff peaks and gently fold them into the batter. Let the batter rest for at least an hour, but preferably overnight.

3. Heat the waffle maker according to the manufacturer's directions. Brush with a little oil and spoon the batter onto the waffle iron. Cook for 4–5 minutes, or until golden. Keep each waffle warm, under aluminum foil and in a low oven, until you are ready to serve.

4. Serve each waffle immediately, topped with yogurt, fig quarters, blackberries, and agave syrup.

WHY NOT TRY

Vary the fruit you use to add different flavours and different levels of sweetness, whilst also providing a healthier edge to the dessert.

Crème Caramel

Sweet, smooth, and ideal as a light dessert, the eggs aid the characteristic silkiness of a crème caramel.

SERVES:	PREP: *25 mins, plus chilling & cooling*	PER SERVING: *377 cals* | *12.7g fat* | *6.1g sat fat* | *57.5g carbs* | *56.7g sugar*
4	COOK: *1 hr 10 mins–1 hr 25 mins*	*0.3g fiber* | *9.7g protein* | *120mg sodium*

INGREDIENTS

1 tablespoon butter, for greasing

1 cup superfine sugar

¼ cup water

½ lemon

2 cups milk

1 vanilla bean

2 extra-large eggs

2 extra-large egg yolks

1. Preheat the oven to 325°F. Lightly grease the bottom and sides of four ramekin dishes. To make the caramel, put ⅓ cup of the sugar with the water into a saucepan over medium–high heat and cook, stirring, until the sugar dissolves. Boil until the syrup turns a deep golden brown. Immediately remove from the heat and squeeze in a few drops of lemon juice. Divide evenly among the ramekin dishes.

2. Pour the milk into a saucepan. Halve the vanilla bean lengthwise and, using the tip of a knife, scrape out the seeds into the milk. Drop the vanilla bean in as well. Bring to a boil, remove the saucepan from the heat, and stir in the remaining sugar, stirring until it dissolves. Reserve.

3. Beat the eggs and yolks together in a bowl and pour the milk mixture over them, whisking. Remove the vanilla bean. Strain the mixture into a bowl and divide evenly among the ramekins.

4. Place the dishes in a roasting pan. Carefully pour boiling water into the pan so that it comes two-thirds of the way up the sides of the dishes.

5. Bake in the preheated oven for 1–1¼ hours, or until a knife inserted in the center comes out clean. Let cool completely. Cover with plastic wrap and let chill in the refrigerator for at least 24 hours.

6. Run a blunt knife around the edge of each dish. Place an up-turned serving plate, with a rim, on top of each dish, then invert the plate and dish, held together, giving a sharp shake halfway over. Lift off the ramekin dishes and serve immediately.

Apricot & Rosemary Clafoutis

This baked French dessert is a comforting, sweet treat, easy to prepare and ideal straight from the oven.

SERVES:	PREP: *20–25 mins*
6	COOK: *25 mins*

PER SERVING: *469 cals* | *26.8g fat* | *15.2g sat fat* | *48.5g carbs* | *35.9g sugar*
1.4g fiber | *9.2g protein* | *80mg sodium*

INGREDIENTS

1 tablespoon butter

¾ cup superfine sugar, plus 2 tablespoons for dusting

2 cups halved and pitted apricots

6 eggs, beaten

1 cup heavy cream

1 teaspoon finely chopped fresh rosemary

¾ cup all-purpose flour, sifted

1. Preheat the oven to 400°F. Grease a large, oval gratin dish, about 10½ inches in diameter, with the butter and dust with 1 tablespoon of sugar.

2. Spread the apricots evenly, cut-side up, over the bottom of the prepared dish and set aside.

3. In a large bowl, whisk the eggs, cream, and ¾ cup of sugar together with the rosemary until light and fluffy, then fold in the flour. Pour the batter carefully over the apricots, being careful not to dislodge them.

4. Bake in the preheated oven for 25 minutes, or until puffed up and set. Dust with the remaining sugar and serve warm or at room temperature.

TOP TIP

Put the gratin dish with the apricots on a baking sheet before you add the batter. This way it is easier to transfer to the oven without spilling the batter or upsetting the layout of the fruit.

Essential Equipment

There are many different gadgets available to help with cooking eggs. Your choice of these will depend on your budget, how you like to use and cook with eggs, and how much storage space you have in your kitchen.

EGG SEPARATOR

These simple devices come in various guises. They separate the yolks from the whites and prevent the shell from breaking into the egg. These are really useful if you like making meringues.

EGG CODDLER

Coddled eggs are gently steamed eggs cooked in specially designed ceramic pots with lids that seal tightly to keep out moisture. The coddlers are lightly buttered before the eggs are added with a little cream and seasoning. The coddlers are then placed in a saucepan of boiling water and simmered for 4 minutes. The pan is removed from the heat and the coddlers stand for about 6 minutes. You could substitute ramekin dishes and cover them with aluminum foil, but egg coddlers are neat and tidy.

POACHING DEVICES

Of course, you can poach eggs without any gadgets, just by adding an egg to a saucepan of boiling water, but if you want guaranteed perfection, then try one of the many devices available to help with the task. These take two main forms: either a shallow saucepan with four removable pods to hold the eggs, or individual silicone egg poaching pods that can be added to a saucepan of boiling water. You can also poach eggs in the microwave, using specially designed lidded containers.

TIMING DEVICES

Again, there are plenty to choose from. Whether it's a traditional timer with sand or a color-changing egg-shape timer to go in the saucepan, which will tell you when your egg is cooked, the choice is yours.

EGG PRICKER

This little device is essentially a stand with a small pin at the bottom onto which the egg is gently pressed. The hole is small enough that the egg won't run out but means that the shell shouldn't break during cooking.

EGG COOKER

An electric timed gadget that cooks the eggs by steaming them in their shells until soft- or hard-boiled, or poaching them to perfection in a mold.

SILICONE/METAL EGG COOKING RINGS

These simply hold the eggs in shape while they cook in the skillet, for those of you who love all things perfect. Otherwise, if you usually fry only a single egg, you could invest in an individual egg pan.

BOILED EGG TOPPER

If you struggle with cutting the tops from freshly boiled eggs, then these are a great idea. They come in a variety of types, and take the top cleanly off the egg .

EGG SPOON

If you're a real lover of soft-boiled eggs, then this is for you. Designed specifically for eating boiled eggs, it has a shorter handle, slightly more pointed tip, and a deeper bowl than a teaspoon, making it easier to get into the egg.

CRÈME BRÛLÉE

This dessert has long been a favorite of many people because the ingredients work in perfect harmony to produce a mouthwatering dish.

SERVES: 6	PREP: *25 mins, plus cooling* COOK: *45–60 mins*

PER SERVING: *510 cals* | *44.1g fat* | *26.3g sat fat* | *24.6g carbs* | *23.9g sugar* *trace fiber* | *4.1g protein* | *trace sodium*

INGREDIENTS

2 cups heavy cream

1 vanilla bean

½ cup superfine sugar, plus 2 tablespoons for the topping

6 egg yolks

1. Preheat the oven to 325°F.

2. Pour the cream into a small saucepan. Cut the vanilla bean in half lengthwise. Scrape the seeds into the pan, then chop the bean into little pieces and add them, too. Heat the cream to boiling, then reduce the heat and simmer gently for 5 minutes.

3. Put the sugar and egg yolks into a heatproof bowl and beat with a spoon until well mixed. Pour the hot cream into the egg mixture, beating (not whisking) as you pour, until thickened. Pass this custard through a fine strainer into another bowl. Pour the mixture into a wide, flat dish and lay it in a roasting pan. Carefully pour boiling water into the pan so that it comes halfway up the sides of the crème brûlée dish.

4. Place in the preheated oven and bake for 30–45 minutes, or until the custard has just set.

5. Remove from the oven and let cool to room temperature. Sprinkle some sugar over the custard and then gently caramelize it, using a kitchen blow torch or under a hot broiler. Let cool for a few minutes then serve.

Classic Meringues

Light and fluffy like clouds, these meringues are topped with a sweet, creamy topping and fresh strawberries.

MAKES:	PREP: *35 mins, plus cooling*	PER TOPPED MERINGUE: *289 cals* | *14.4g fat* | *8.9g sat fat* | *38.5g carbs*
10	COOK: *1 hr 10 mins*	*36.5g sugar* | *1g fiber* | *2.3g protein* | *trace sodium*

INGREDIENTS

4 egg whites

1½ cups superfine sugar

2 teaspoons white wine vinegar

2 teaspoons cornstarch

1¼ cups heavy cream

¼ cup confectioners' sugar

1 teaspoon vanilla extract

3 cups hulled strawberries (halved if large)

1. Preheat the oven to 350°F. Put a round cutter on top of a sheet of parchment paper and carefully trace around it with a pencil. Draw five circles on one sheet and repeat on another sheet. Put each parchment paper, drawn side down, on a baking sheet.

2. Put the egg whites in a large bowl and whisk, using an electric hand mixer, until the egg whites stand in firm, stiff peaks.

3. Whisk in the superfine sugar, a tablespoonful at a time, until the mixture is shiny and stiff, then whisk in the vinegar and cornstarch.

4. Spoon the mixture onto the circles on the parchment paper and make a dip in the center of each with the back of the spoon.

5. Bake for 10 minutes, then turn the oven down to 250°F and cook for 1 hour. Remove from the oven and let the meringues cool a little, then move to a wire rack.

6. Whisk together the cream, confectioners' sugar, and vanilla extract in another large bowl until the mixture stands in soft peaks. Spoon the cream into the dips in the meringues and top with strawberries.

Tiramisù

This classic Italian dessert is always a winner. This version is made with mascarpone cheese, but for a healthier version you could use low-fat cream cheese.

SERVES:	PREP: *25–30 mins, plus chilling*	PER SERVING: *619 cals* | *40.4g fat* | *27.5g sat fat* | *43.8g carbs* | *34.1g sugar*
6	COOK: *5 mins*	*1.3g fiber* | *8.3g protein* | *80mg sodium*

INGREDIENTS

4 egg yolks
½ cup superfine sugar
1 teaspoon vanilla extract
2 cups mascarpone cheese
2 egg whites
¾ cup strong black coffee
½ cup rum or brandy
24 ladyfingers
2 tablespoons unsweetened cocoa powder
2 tablespoons finely grated semisweet chocolate

1. Whisk the egg yolks with the sugar and vanilla extract in a heatproof bowl set over a saucepan of barely simmering water.

2. When the mixture is pale and the whisk or beaters leave a ribbon trail when lifted, remove the bowl from the heat and set aside to cool. Whisk occasionally to prevent a skin from forming.

3. When the egg yolk mixture is cool, beat in the mascarpone until thoroughly combined.

4. Whisk the egg whites in a separate, clean bowl until they form soft peaks, then gently fold them into the mascarpone mixture.

5. Combine the coffee and rum in a shallow dish. Briefly dip eight of the ladyfingers in the liquid, then arrange in the bottom of a deep, wide serving dish.

6. Spoon one-third of the mascarpone mixture on top, spreading it out evenly. Repeat the layers twice, finishing with the mascarpone mixture. Chill in the refrigerator for at least 1 hour.

7. Sift the cocoa evenly over the top and sprinkle with the chocolate. Serve immediately.

Baked Lemon Cheesecake

Eggs are vital in making this cheesecake as smooth and creamy as it can be, whilst the lemons provide a tangy edge to balance the sweetness.

SERVES:	PREP: *25 mins, plus chilling*
8	COOK: *45 mins*

PER SERVING: *353 cals | 24.1g fat | 11.9g sat fat | 31.2g carbs | 20.6g sugar 1.2g fiber | 11.5g protein | 160mg sodium*

INGREDIENTS

4 tablespoons butter, plus 1 tablespoon for greasing
1½ cups crushed gingersnaps
3 lemons
1¼ cups ricotta cheese
1 cup Greek-style yogurt
4 eggs
1 tablespoon cornstarch
½ cup superfine sugar
strips of lemon zest, to decorate (optional)

1. Preheat the oven to 350°F. Grease an 8-inch round springform cake pan and line with parchment paper.

2. Melt the butter and stir in the cookie crumbs. Press into the bottom of the prepared cake pan. Chill in the refrigerator until firm.

3. Meanwhile, finely grate the zest and squeeze the juice from the lemons. Add the ricotta, yogurt, eggs, cornstarch, and superfine sugar, and whisk until a smooth batter is formed.

4. Carefully spoon the mixture into the pan. Bake in the preheated oven for 40–45 minutes, or until just firm and golden brown.

5. Cool the cheesecake completely in the pan, then run a knife around the edge to loosen and transfer to a serving plate. Decorate with strips of lemon zest, if using, and serve.

Lemon Angel Food Cake

Some say this light and airy sponge cake originated in India. However, many Southern Americans believe that a frugal ancestor created the cake to avoid discarding egg whites left over from other recipes.

SERVES:	PREP: *25–30 mins, plus cooling*	PER SERVING: *168 cals*	*0.6g fat*	*trace sat fat*	*35.3g carbs*	*25.3g sugar*
10	COOK: *35–45 mins*	*0.2g fiber*	*5.3g protein*	*120mg sodium*

INGREDIENTS

12 egg whites
1¼ teaspoons cream of tartar
pinch of salt
1–1½ cups sugar
1 cup cake flour, sifted
1 teaspoon lemon extract
½ teaspoon vanilla extract

1. Preheat the oven to 350°F. Beat the egg whites with a handheld electric mixer on high speed until light and foamy. Add the cream of tartar and salt and beat again until they hold soft peaks.

2. Add the sugar, 2 tablespoons at a time, beating until the mixture holds stiff peaks. Sprinkle the flour into the mixture, a little at a time, folding in each addition carefully. Fold in the lemon extract and vanilla extract.

3. Pour the batter into an ungreased 10-inch mold pan, spreading it evenly. Bake in the preheated oven for 35–45 minutes, or until the cake springs back when lightly touched.

4. Remove the cake from the oven and immediately invert the pan onto a wire rack. Let cool for at least 1 hour, then remove the cake from the pan and serve.

WHY NOT TRY

Use 1–1½ teaspoons of fresh lemon juice instead of lemon extract, if you prefer. For an extra lemony twist, also add 1½ teaspoons of freshly grated lemon zest, along with the juice.

Goan Layered Coconut Cake

This traditional Goan dessert is best served warm with ice cream and it can be preserved for a long time, so nothing goes to waste!

SERVES:	PREP: *35 mins, plus chilling*
10	COOK: *1 hr 50 mins–2 hrs 15 mins*

PER SERVING: *406 cals | 22.5g fat | 15.1g sat fat | 47.2g carbs | 31.1g sugar*
0.6g fiber | 5.7g protein | 80mg sodium

INGREDIENTS

1¾ cups coconut milk
1½ cups superfine sugar
10 egg yolks, lightly beaten
1⅔ cups all-purpose flour
½ teaspoon freshly grated nutmeg
1 teaspoon freshly ground cardamom seeds
pinch of ground cloves
¼ teaspoon ground cinnamon
1 stick butter, plus 1 tablespoon for greasing

1. Preheat the oven to 400°F. Lightly grease a 6½-inch nonstick, round cake pan and line with parchment paper.

2. Pour the coconut milk into a saucepan and stir in the sugar. Heat gently for 8–10 minutes, stirring until the sugar has dissolved. Remove from the heat and gradually add the beaten egg yolks, whisking all the time so that the eggs do not scramble and the mixture is smooth. Sift in the flour and spices and stir to make a smooth batter.

3. Melt the butter, then add a tablespoon to the prepared pan and spread over the bottom. Pour one-eighth of the batter into the pan and spread to coat the bottom evenly. Bake in the preheated oven for 10–12 minutes, or until set.

4. Remove from the oven and brush another spoonful of the melted butter over the top, followed by another eighth of the batter. Return to the oven and cook for 10–12 minutes, or until set.

5. Repeat this process until all the butter and batter has been used, baking for an additional 20–25 minutes, or until the top is golden brown and the cake is firmly set. Remove from the oven and let cool in the pan.

6. When cool, remove from the pan, cover with plastic wrap, and chill for 4–6 hours before serving.

Raspberry & Mascarpone Ice Cream

Fresh raspberries and extra creaminess from the mascarpone mean you may be fighting people off the last scoops of this delicious ice cream.

SERVES:	PREP: *25 mins, plus freezing*
8	COOK: *5–10 mins*

PER SERVING: *285 cals | 28.6g fat | 16.5g sat fat | 3.9g carbs | 1.2g sugar 0.8g fiber | 4.2g protein | 40mg sodium*

INGREDIENTS

1 extra-large egg, plus 4 extra-large egg yolks
2½ tablespoons stevia (sugar substitute)
½ cup mascarpone cheese
1 teaspoon vanilla extract
1½ cups heavy cream
⅔ cup halved raspberries

1. Crack the egg into a large heatproof bowl, add the yolks and stevia, and beat with an electric handheld mixer for 30 seconds. Put over a saucepan of gently simmering water, making sure the bowl doesn't touch the water, and whisk until the mixture is pale and airy. This cooks the eggs and makes a sweet custard, but be careful not to overcook it.

2. To cool the custard, pour cold water into a large bowl and put the custard bowl into it, so that its bottom is in the water. Continue to whisk for 2 minutes, then lift the bowl out of the water and set aside.

3. Put the mascarpone and vanilla in another large bowl and beat briefly until loose. Pour in the cream and beat again until it forms soft peaks.

4. Using a metal spoon, gently fold the custard into the cream mixture, preserving as much air as possible. Stir in the raspberries.

5. Pour the mixture into a freezer-proof container, cover with a lid, and freeze for 4 hours, or until set. Take the ice cream out of the freezer 10 minutes before you serve it to let it soften. Scoop it into glasses or small bowls and serve immediately.

HELPFUL HINT

To make it even easier to scoop out the ice cream, put your ice-cream scoop in a jug of hot water for a couple of minutes before using it.

Index